Profiles in Success

Profiles in Success

Inspiration from Executive Leaders

Volume 1

GORDON J. BERNHARDT, CPA, PFS, CFP®, AIF®

ISBN: 978-0-9972483-7-1

First edition

Gordon Bernhardt conducts interviews of business leaders primarily in the Washington D.C. area who come recommended by their peers. The profiles included in this volume are a result of these interviews. As a result of these additional insights Mr. Bernhardt has published these profiles. Gordon Bernhardt is the President and CEO of Bernhardt Wealth Management, a registered investment adviser with the Securities and Exchange Commission. Registration is mandatory for all persons meeting the definition of investment adviser and does not imply a certain level of skill or training. The business leaders may or may not be clients of Bernhardt Wealth Management. These interviews are independent of investment advisory services and do not imply any endorsement of Gordon Bernhardt or Bernhardt Wealth Management by the business leaders.

This book exists because of all the inspirational individuals who so graciously shared their stories with me. I am thankful for the opportunity to get to know each and every one of you. I feel like a better person thanks to what I learned from you and your story.

To my team at Bernhardt Wealth Management—Tim Koehl, Bonnie Armstrong, and Emily Burns. I would never have been able to do this without your efforts and support throughout the process. Thank you for all you do for each other and for our clients.

I am deeply grateful to Marie Swift, President and CEO of Impact Communications, Inc., and to Peter Schwartz, Master Chair of Vistage Worldwide, for your help and encouragement on this project. Thank you.

And lastly, this book would not have been possible without the guidance and creative support of Karen Embry.

Table of Contents

Foreword

Taken root from the popular Executive Leaders Radio broadcasts Gordon Bernhardt shares the stories and wisdom of successful business leaders with the goal of helping others achieve the same level of success.

While headlines scream the stories of corporate greed and misconduct, Gordon understood that there are many more executives in the business world whose stories are positive and even motivating. Those are the stories that interested him and those are the stories he chose to profile in order to celebrate the entrepreneurial spirit and inspire future business leaders.

Gordon J. Bernhardt, president and founder of Bernhardt Wealth Management, is himself a successful business leader. Gordon provides strategic investment management and financial planning counsel to his clients. Gordon recognizes that while fulfilling work is important, the greatest rewards come from living a well-rounded life. For that reason, he strives to relieve his clients of their financial anxieties, so that they can pursue their dreams.

Gordon prides himself on being a fiduciary advisor which means he goes beyond the minimum requirements of the suitability standard. As a fiduciary he is legally bound to put his clients' best interests first. That includes only selecting and recommending products in the investors' best interest; either avoid or completely disclose any conflicts of interest; before beginning work, explain all compensation, incentives, commissions and expenses; ensure expenses are fair and reasonable; and do only what is best for the investor.

My team and I have thoroughly enjoyed working with Gordon to assemble his collection of case studies. Our admiration for him as a humble, yet successful and well-respected professional has grown exponentially throughout this process. We are proud to be associated with such a worthwhile project. I know you will enjoy reading his books and sharing them with others!

– **Marie Swift**
President and CEO
Impact Communications, Inc.
www.ImpactCommunications.org

Since entering the financial services industry in 1991, Marie Swift has worked with some of the best and brightest financial advisors in the nation. She has been a columnist for major trade publications such as Financial Planning magazine, Research magazine and Morningstar Advisor. Her firm also represents and has worked with dozens of nationally recognized companies such as Fina-Metrica Risk Profiling Software, TD Ameritrade Institutional, Kinder Institute of Life Planning, National Association of Personal Financial Advisors, Pershing, Schwab Advisor Services, fi360 and many more.

Introduction

Working to Reconnect and Rebuild Trust

Maybe you've heard the expression, "Trust is the hardest thing to earn and the easiest thing to lose." Any kind of relationship without trust is in trouble. Having been through some history-making turbulent times during the past three years,many Americans have lost faith in institutions they formally viewed as trustworthy—the media and big business, even our nation's government and religious organizations. In particular, in recent years, corporate greed and lax risk management policies at the nation's largest financial institutions and high-profile Ponzi schemes have resulted in a significant erosion of trust from Wall Street to Main Street. With the essential bonds of trust frayed, suspicion and disbelief permeate our personal and professional relationships.

While it seems like this widespread mistrust occurred overnight, in reality, it was a long time coming. Over time, factors ranging from suburban sprawl to our increasing reliance on technology have combined to create an isolationism that leaves many citizens unsure how they fit into their communities. Sadly, rather than participate in elections, volunteer in the community, or simply greet a next door neighbor, many Americans are content to retreat to their homes and engage with the world through their television or computer. Far less involved with our communities than our grandparents were, our isolationism makes us more inclined to mistrust others, individuals as well as institutions.

Of course, the highly publicized crimes and misdeeds of Bernie Madoff and British Petroleum, among many other individuals and institutions, only serve to convince inward looking individuals that putting their trust in any professional or government official will result in betrayal. That is, the more we hear about wrongdoings and unethical behavior, the more we feel justified in withdrawing from our community and withholding our trust.

As a farm boy from Nebraska who grew up in a close-knit community where your word was your bond, a personal connection to both my community and my work has always been integral to my happiness. Early in my career when I worked as an auditor, I knew the information I provided was essential to investors, yet I didn't feel like I was adding true value. Years later, when I transitioned to the wealth management industry, I realized it was the satisfaction I gained from interacting with clients one-on-one, and doing all I could to help them reach their goals, that was missing from my previous work.

Why I Wrote This Book

Today, even in the wake of the Great Recession, I enjoy trusting and productive long-term relationships with a wonderful group of clients. And, through my involvement with Executive Leaders Radio (ExecutiveLeadersRadio.com), I'm working to help other small business owners to become similarly successful. By interviewing a diverse group of small business owners and sharing their words of wisdom, our program strives to help local executives connect with leaders their community, learn from the successes and innovation of others, and cultivate the trust that remains the bedrock of all successful client relationships. Further, by creating a venue that celebrates business owners and executives who conduct themselves in an ethical and commendable fashion, we hope to counter the negative stories of corporate theft and deception we are all too accustomed to finding on the front page.

Executive Leaders Radio has been very well received by the public. The shows serve several million listeners in Pennsylvania, New Jersey, Delaware, Maryland, Washington D.C. and Virginia, broadcasting frequently on WHAT AM-1340, WCHE AM-1520, WYFL AM-1180, WNWR AM-1540, WHFS AM-1580 and internationally on AOL-Radio.com, YahooRadio.com, SBNonline, PodcastAlley, SmartCEO and iTunes. Because they are carried on two of the three largest international internet radio stations—the #1 AOL radio and the #3 Yahoo Radio—the interviews can be listened to by 7 million people, not only in the United States, but also in many foreign countries.

Recently, I decided to expand on the short radio interviews to produce written case studies on various radio guests. The entrepreneurialism and positive spirit expressed by the inspiring men and women profiled for this collection reflect the talent and hope our nation needs for a complete economic recovery. Even with the recession and credit crunch taking a heavy toll on U.S. small businesses, they remain the backbone of our country. Remember, according to the U.S. Small Business Administration, the 27.2 million small businesses across the country employ nearly half of our nation's workforce and produce a great many innovations. Small business is critical to our economic recovery and for securing our nation's place in the increasingly competitive global marketplace.

I intend to share this collection with business people as well as students at local universities and business schools. It's my hope that in addition to offering insight into management techniques and tools, these compelling success stories will illuminate career paths for students. Above all, I hope that the successes chronicled here will inspire today's college students to pursue their personal passions so that the entrepreneurial spirit that our country was built on can continue to thrive.

I hope you will enjoy these profiles as much as I enjoyed getting to know these business people and telling their stories. If you know a local business owner worthy of a future profile, please feel free to contact me. I look forward to expanding this collection in order to help build connections and foster trust in our local business community.

– **Gordon J. Bernhardt, CPA, PFS, CFP®, AIF®**
Founder, President and CEO
Bernhardt Wealth Management, Inc.
www.BernhardtWealth.com

Since establishing his firm in 1994, Gordon Bernhardt has been focused on providing high-quality service and independent financial advice in order to help his clients make smart decisions about their money. He specializes in addressing the unique needs of successful professionals, entrepreneurs and retirees, as well as women in transition throughout the Washington, DC area. Over the years, Gordon has been sought out by numerous media outlets including MSN Money, CNN Money, Kiplinger and The New York Times for his insight into subjects related to personal finance.

Profiles

Michelle Boggs

The Goal to Give Back

"Well, Mount McKinley is the tallest peak in North America," came Amanda Weathersby's voice through the phone.

Michelle Boggs considered this a moment. It was a somewhat relaxed Saturday morning, and the two business partners were batting around names for the new marketing consulting firm they were preparing to launch. The symbolic element in the suggestion was certainly appealing—the size, strength, and majesty of the highest mountain in the country would be hard to beat.

"Tying the company to a national landmark like that would be so fitting, too, because marketing is as American as apple pie," Amanda added. Michelle agreed, and thus, McKinley Marketing Partners was named.

McKinley was founded as a spinoff from Amanda's company, The Weathersby Group, which had a parallel focus and was launched in

1991. At the time, Michelle was running a nonprofit that was proving difficult to fund when she read about Amanda and her business model in the Washington Post. Fascinated by the concept, she contacted the entrepreneur with characteristic proactive diligence. Amanda was originally hoping to hire Michelle to work in business development but happened to hear about a project that would be perfect for her new acquaintance's skill set, so Michelle instead assumed the role of an independent contractor. However, despite working on various projects for Amanda throughout the next three years, she still had the opportunity to participate in the business development aspect of the company more intimately than most contractors would.

The unique knowledge Michelle acquired through experiencing both facets of the company in this manner was suddenly thrust into the spotlight when the Telecommunications Act of 1996 was first being discussed. The reform would escalate competition between the various telecom companies, and Amanda wanted to keep a low profile in order to maintain peace and good relations. Michelle, however, saw the tremendous value in the changing landscape, and the two women joined with one other partner to create McKinley with the idea that it would service other telecom groups not yet associated with Weathersby. Since then, Michelle has acquired full ownership of the firm, which is headquartered in the DC metro area but has also opened offices in Dallas and New York.

From the time of its inception in 1995, the company has lived up to its namesake, gaining repute and growth through its service to the commercial sector and primarily the Fortune 500 companies that look to it for support and insight. These are companies with robust marketing divisions who look to McKinley not to outsource their needs, but rather to fill gaps when their workload exceeds their capacity for whatever reason. McKinley, in turn, supplies marketing professionals that have served in corporate America as employees but hope to transition into independent contractors. Though ninety-eight percent of their business draws from interim or project work, they do facilitate permanent placement when requested.

Likewise, McKinley does supply strategic marketing planning and project development services, but these more generalized requests are somewhat rare. Rather, when a client approaches Michelle's company, they typically have a clear and detailed idea of the type of skill set they seek. McKinley then draws upon its database of available contractors. The system holds comprehensive demographic and professional information of between three and four hundred contacts at any given time with the intent that any proposed requirement can be filled promptly and, true to Michelle's perfectionist nature, ideally. "We match the skill set and what looks good on paper, but we also make sure it's a cultural fit," she explains. "This is why it's so important for us to get to know the client and their culture in advance so, when a requirement does come in, we'll be able to match more efficiently and effectively." Conversely, McKinley is highly selective in terms of its contractors and screens each of its candidates rigorously before accepting an individual into their database as an Interim Marketing Manager (IMM).

In addition to its ironclad methodology, McKinley is highly unique in the fact of its ultra-specialization. While more and more publicly traded staffing companies are carving out a marketing services arm, McKinley is among the only firms dedicated solely to the industry. "This specialization may sound narrow, but the world of marketing is actually far more diverse than many people realize," Michelle points out. "We have fifty-five marketing specialties under our own umbrella—product, product marketing, product development, communications, public relations, public affairs, etc. Furthermore, all these components have either a business-to-business or business-to-consumer element." She also acknowledges online and digital marketing, which is in a state of perpetual evolution and progress. Focusing specifically on marketing consulting allows McKinley to be at the top of its game, able to offer their clients the most fresh and innovative solutions.

The company's high functionality is further enabled through its proprietary database, McKinley Information Management System. The tool is the centerpiece of the firm's organization and infrastructure, maintaining their recruiting, requirement management, and project management elements through a very intuitive and synchronized technology. All of this is accomplished through a web-based interface, which Michelle fortuitously invested in long before the technology was popular. The database boasts the robustness typically found only in larger companies, allowing McKinley to remain competitive and efficient even when operating with a fairly lean staff. "You must be willing to invest in the tools, processes, and procedures that will allow your team to succeed," Michelle explains. "Without the customization of our database, we would still be flying by the seat of our pants the way we were back when I was doing everything myself. You just can't grow and sustain that way."

This resolute commitment to firm foundational processes seems to resemble the kind of practice-makes-perfect attitude demonstrated by many serious athletes, which makes sense considering Michelle's sports-infused history. She had been an avid tennis player throughout high school and college, later working with World Championship Tennis, headquartered in Dallas from 1984 to 1987. She was then recruited by ProServ, an internationally acclaimed sports management firm, to run their men's senior tennis tour, which proved to be no small feat. She reflects on this period of her life as a defining epoch in terms of skill development and business experience. From public relations to site selection management to negotiating with promoters, sponsors, and players, she got her feet wet in virtually every aspect of the leadership and management. "They really just threw me in, and it was great training grounds for running a business," she says.

Her affinity to tennis struggled later, however, when she suffered a debilitating skiing accident and was faced with three shoulder surgeries over the span of eighteen months. Through her intensive daily physical therapy sessions, she befriended a mountain climber who had shattered his ankle in a freak accident. When she found out he would soon lose his leg due to a bone infection, Michelle's mind focused around the profound sense of loss echoed in each of their plights. Identifying this underserved societal ill, she decided to create a nonprofit foundation that would provide products and services for elite athletes that suffered psychological and emotional effects after being separated from their sport due to an injury. The foundation, called the Athletic Counseling and Training Institute, would publish an expansive series of newsletters. Each issue would revolve around a specific type of injury through the commentary of doctors, psychologists, and advanced athletes who had suffered and coped with the ailment first-hand.

Though the project was underwritten for several test issues and received ample positive feedback, Michelle attributes the lack of funding that ensued to the fear and uncertainty generated through Clinton's health care reform proposal. She remained committed to the fledgling organization as she earned a living through consulting for Weathersby, but in the end she sensed that her calling lay down a different path. Had she not pursued this path, McKinley would not exist today.

This is not to suggest, however, that Michelle's commitment and future plans do not remain steadfastly committed to serving a greater good. In truth, her next endeavor will most likely be charitably inclined. Though she had been mentally developing a business plan for such a project for quite some time, she originally felt as though she had to wait until other goals were accomplished—namely, selling McKinley to the appropriate buyer. After recently meeting entrepreneur and philanthropist Ted Leonsis, however, she was particularly compelled by the sense of urgency inherent in his idea of corporate social responsibility. This influence led her to the invaluable realization that nothing was stopping her from making her move today. "I intend to launch an initiative in which a certain portion of our clients' payments goes directly to a charity of their choosing," she says excitedly. She hopes to start the initiative by funneling donations to organizations supporting women and children in need. Contractors would have the opportunity to donate as well, and each participant would be able to track the sum of their contributions through McKinley's website. "Ultimately, then, I hope to leave the professional legacy that I gave more than I got," says Michelle, quoting Leonsis.

To young entrepreneurs entering the workplace today, Michelle cautions about the stark divide between campus life and the business realm. "College certainly teaches you the discipline of learning, but it doesn't prepare you for the real world," she explains. How does one, then, adequately prepare for the rat race? While she feels that getting an MBA should provide substantial advantage, there is also much to be said for learning from those close to you. From an early age, for example, Michelle had the privilege of observing her stepfather, who was a serial entrepreneur with many failures, some successes, and then one big success later on. Competitive by nature and fueled by his example, Michelle had made it her goal to start her own business by age thirty. The fact that she was five years behind her preordained schedule hardly matters in light of the fact that her goal was, in fact, so successfully accomplished. With her history of achievement, then, one can optimistically look toward Michelle's future as one with tremendous potential for continued enrichment as she strives to spin get into give.

Mary Lynne Carraway

The World's Trials, The Soul's Triumphs

What is the measure of a story? Is it the distance scaled between the point at which it begins and the point at which it ends? If that were the case, one might get the impression that Mary Lynne Carraway's life has been a straight line connecting these two points, when nothing could be further from the truth. In truth, the events that separate the four-year-old waitress drawing her customers' orders in crayon from the woman who won the Circle of Excellence Award as one of Washington, D.C.'s top ten CEOs in 2010 dip even as they soar. They show us, more than any made-up fairy tale or fabricated anecdote could, how being true to one's self and one's convictions can weave the greatest trials into the greatest triumphs. "If you try to live your life in accordance with the principles you feel to be true in your soul, I really believe that you'll find your place and everything you need," Mary Lynne describes. "Your story is unique to only you, and you can become anything you want to be. Things you thought would stop you in your tracks are forgivable and surmountable, so don't give up."

With the moral of the story in mind, let us flip back to a different beginning, a different ending. Twenty-five years ago, a young man named Frank Meeks made the move from Mississippi to Washington, D.C. to attend law school. Strapped for cash, he got a job delivering pizzas for extra money but soon realized how valuable the business was and instead launched his own Dominos Pizza franchise. Everyone said the product wouldn't catch on in D.C., but Frank was soon able to add a couple more stores to his repertoire. It wasn't until Frank's story intersected with David Carraway's, however, that things really changed.

David was a graduate of the University of Southern Mississippi who had come to Washington to work on a political campaign. Frank and David had been fraternity brothers, and after reconnecting at a fraternity fundraising event in DC, Frank persuaded him to join his team. David then worked through the MIT Manager-In-Training Program and soon became manager of his own store before vaulting into the position of Vice President. Together, Frank and David built Domino's Team Washington to sixty stores and over 1,400 employees, making them among the most successful franchisees in Domino's history.

Enter Mary Lynne, a young woman raised in rural Pennsylvania with a past that was just as interesting as her future promised to be. The youngest of seven children, she sensed the true measure of loss at the age of two when the family's house burned down along with all of their possessions. This devastation was further compounded several months later when one of her brothers was killed in a car accident. Clinging to the restaurant they had owned and operated for seventeen years, Mary Lynne's parents had a tenacity and perseverance rarely cultivated in today's generation. "They are people of substance, truly loyal to their cause," Mary Lynne reflects now.

"I was raised in the back room of that restaurant," she says, "coloring during the rush times and then coming out to help when the atmosphere was more laid back." Though she would do dishes, burn garbage, sweep, and mop, her favorite job was packing together the hamburger patties, and she remembers fondly how the sense of necessity drew her family together under the banner of honest hard work for the good of the whole. "We all worked together, and it was the greatest gift my parents could have given us," she emphasizes now.

After her family sold their restaurant when Mary Lynne was fifteen, she continued working for the new owners for a time until she got a job as hostess at a Holiday Inn thirty miles away in Indiana. This was followed by a modeling job on the weekends as she finished up her high school career. Opportunities in the fashion industry began unfolding for the young girl, and after much consideration, she decided to seize the day and leave Brigham Young University after her freshman year to pursue them in Chicago.

It was around this time that Mary Lynne flew out to Washington, DC to join her parents on a trip when she was stricken with appendicitis, forcing her to put her modeling career on hold and head in another direction. Resolving to stay in the area, she got a job as the manager of a Marriot Hotel and moved to Gaithersburg, Maryland.

A strong believer in the Mormon faith, she later signed up for a mission trip and was in the midst of her preparations when she met David Carraway. "Getting married and having children was always a focal goal of mine," she explains, tracing this ambition back to the tremendous love and support she enjoyed as a child from her own family. A non-Mormon, David didn't fit into the mold she had always imagined for herself. Instead, he inspired Mary Lynne to love outside the lines of her own expectations.

Free to move around and experience living in D.C., New York, Paris, and Chicago, the young couple enjoyed happiness and prosperity save for one setback: their inability to have the children they had always dreamed of. They adopted their first daughter, Molly, and then learned of a European doctor who had developed a brand new fertility treatment with great promise. Through a fortuitous series of events, Mary Lynne was able to be among the first U.S. patients to undergo the procedure, resulting in the miracle of her first son, Carson. The blessing was replicated over the following years with the births of Brandon and then Hannah, filling the Carraway house with the abundant love it had yearned for so dearly.

"In a way, I think many of our greatest trials are uniquely made for us to serve as real tests," she reflects. "Tests of faith, tests of trying to understand it all. And even though it's hard, it always comes back to what I know is true and good about this life and beyond this life." While her story thus far had certainly helped to outline this ideology, it wasn't until several years later that it was leant more breadth and conviction when Frank Meeks fell gravely ill and David was diagnosed with brain cancer shortly afterward. Dominos lost a wonderful friend and franchisee when Frank then passed away, but with his own cancer in remission, David concentrated his energy on helping Mary Lynne learn the ropes of Team Washington. The family hoped for the best but faced the odds realistically, striving to equip Mary Lynne with the tools she would need to fill the shoes of her mentor and husband if necessary. "It's a mental strength you have to gain through your life," she says now, reflecting on the experience. "It's holding on and enduring—not just enduring, but enduring *well.*"

Despite these proactive strides, Mary Lynne still found herself faced with an advanced-level agility course when David took a tragic turn for the worse. Because Dominos was a comparatively young company, the majority of its leadership was still coming of age, and the sudden loss of such a pivotal figure presented challenges that the young corporation was not prepared to face. Constrained by a web of established policies and practices, Mary Lynne had to assume management of a store and work her way through the ranks, fervently supplementing her work with accelerated accounting classes and the Manager-in-Training Program David had taken. What's more, Frank and David had been awarded seats in Domino's Chairman Circle, among the company's most coveted honors. "For me to step in, a homemaker who had been at home with her children for twenty years, was definitely unprecedented," Mary Lynne recalls. "It was understandably hard on everybody." In the end, however, her efforts paid off, and she was officially named President and CEO of Domino's Team Washington only one week before David passed away.

With four children to support and decent means by which to do so, many people might find the prospect of developing an entirely new range of aptitudes simply out of the question when dealing with the death of a spouse. For Mary Lynne, however, stepping up to the plate her husband had dedicated his life to developing was a no-brainer. "It was a very interesting and trying time, but I always knew I was supposed to do it," she explains. Through David's tremendous passion and commitment to the company, Dominos had truly become part of the Carraway family. "I look at these guys that work for us with great admiration," says Mary Lynne. "David was part of their team, and for many of them, losing him was like losing a brother or a father figure. I knew Frank and David's deaths would either make us pull together or jump ship."

Incredibly, this time of devastating transition didn't drive a single employee from Team Washington's upper management ranks, and as Mary Lynne sits on the Board of Dominos Pizza Worldwide today, other leaders are constantly asking how they might instill the same culture of family and closeness that has always defined the Washington franchises. "I think we really stand out because of what we've been through," she points out. She also promotes the commitment to balance between work life and family life that David himself always maintained, augmenting his approach with her own presence, which lends a calming and peaceful element to an otherwise competitive and thick-skinned industry. Above all, Mary Lynne understands that her employees are people with good days, bad days, and families of their own. She not only embraces this reality, but celebrates and encourages it, ever attuned to the evolving character and needs of both her employees and of the company as a whole.

This respect and appreciation for the softer side of business is infused in the management style and leadership philosophy Mary Lynne strives to enforce every day throughout Team Washington, Inc. Integrity is paramount throughout its franchises in both workers and managers. Ideals like honesty and respect can be difficult to maintain in an environment that can get heated and intense at times, but Mary Lynne expects nothing less from her employees. “I don’t care how intense it gets. Everyone is to be treated humanely and kindly at all times,” she affirms. “David would want us all to learn to be a little kinder, a little gentler.” For her, leading at Dominos through example is just another avenue through which David’s life and work can be kept alive. “When people get distanced from a situation like the loss of David, they tend to forget the lessons that came along with it,” she observes. “Instead, I focus on remembering and conveying them everyday.”

With so much texture to her story, it comes as no surprise that Mary Lynne’s advice to young entrepreneurs maintains the same element of timeless relevance outside of the workplace as it does within a business setting. “From one moment to the next, a bad day can transform into a great day, so don’t get lost in the moment thinking something is too hard to handle,” she says. “Try to be a positive person in all that you do. Not only is this attitude infectious, but it conveys to others that you have the kind of depth that allows you to learn from your hardships rather than shy away from them.” Indeed, it conveys the will not only to live your own story, but to examine it, coming to know and embrace its characters, themes, and morals. It shows the courage it takes to find your own ending, and in that ending, a new beginning from which to persevere.

Todd Chamberlin

Leading Innovation through Family Focus

Struck by a sudden sense of ardent realization, Todd Chamberlin stopped rifling through his father's effects and paused with his hand on the old photograph. He could almost smell the sweat that would soak his shirt after a long day of hard labor under a hot summer sun; could again feel that sense of fulfillment from seeing the look on a customer's face when he'd exceeded their expectations. Even in his first job mowing lawns at age twelve, Todd had always earned generous praise from clients. His father, however, had been a different story. A man with unparalleled work ethic and tight-lipped sternness, Ashby Chamberlin was not apt to dispense expressions of praise or pride despite his son's best efforts. Even after assuming presidency of Kenwood Golf and Country Club in 2005, he still found himself wondering at times if he was living up to his father's unspoken expectations. But here, staring at the photograph that Ashby had kept of the young boy on a bicycle trailing his lawn mower behind him, Todd felt a whole history of commendation wash over him.

If there's one thing that makes Kenwood unique amongst its peers, it's the theme of family that so thoroughly permeates its nature and philosophy. Established in 1928 in Bethesda, Maryland, the 108-acre property became an heirloom of the Chamberlin family in the 1950s when Donal Chamberlin split ways with his business partners and acquired sole ownership of the club. His son, Ashby Chamberlin, got involved with the club at age 26. Todd, coincidentally, also began working at the club at age 26, gaining ample expertise and knowledge to assume the presidency in succession. Now, five years later, he has expanded his family's legacy into a state-of-the-art facility poised at the forefront of its industry. And, if you were to speak with Todd about his aspirations for the future, you'd find he's just getting started.

Not only is Kenwood the only family-owned country club in the area, but its entire business model is oriented around family. While clubs have historically tended to discourage the presence of children and have fostered a "boy's club" atmosphere, the country club landscape is shifting toward more family-friendly practices, and Kenwood appears to be ahead of the trend. Its emphasis on children is reflected in the various activities, events, and seasonal camps offered by the club, as well as by the welcoming and tolerant attitude of the staff and members. Kenwood has positioned itself as a place where families can spend quality time together, and the vision has paid off tremendously through the satisfaction of its membership, which holds at around sixteen hundred.

While the theme of family has remained pervasive throughout Kenwood's history, Todd's management philosophy has initiated a new era for the club. Whereas Ashby Chamberlin's method tended toward the preservation and maintenance of the club's unique charm, Todd hoped to offer new and innovative amenities to its members and redesigned its budget such that initiation fees were used for improvements rather than subsidization. The centerpiece of this visionary and disciplined approach and of his presidency to date is the club's extraordinary fitness center, which features a 75-yard swimming pool, full-service spa and locker rooms, group exercise room, childcare facilities, and an eighteen-person Jacuzzi. Serving as a gathering place for family and friends, the fitness center upholds the club's deepest values while also offering an ideal product in light of the fact that the American College of Sports Medicine has ranked DC as the most health-conscious city in America. Todd credits the fidelity of Kenwood's membership in spite of the current recession in large part to this feature.

But not just *any* fitness center could serve as a sticking point for clientele when deciding whether to retain their membership or not. In the early 2000s, companies generally built more conservative fitness centers, which are now the chief complaint of members in today's club landscape. Had Todd followed this trend, he would now be faced with the need to upgrade a past project instead of focusing on new ones. In planning for the center, he intended to construct a facility that would remain competitive for three or four decades, he reports. So far, this goal has been realized.

So how exactly does one come to acquire this intuitive degree of forward-thinking? Todd argues that it is not bred from intuition at all, but rather from instinct—survival instinct, to be more specific. Even from the time of his lawn mowing ventures, he felt an inner drive toward the achievement of self-sufficiency and independence. He had adopted the tremendous work ethic of his father—a man who, as Todd explains, can still outwork most people even at the age of seventy-two. Compelled by this sense of discipline, he worked hard as a boy and came to understand that his own survival and independence was inextricably linked to his ability to foster truthful and genuine relationships with his customers. Thus, excellent client service was set as a cornerstone of his management philosophy and has proven to be a strong foundation for his role at Kenwood.

Patience and understanding, Todd explains, are the other crucial traits to possess from the time one first enters the workforce. In his early affiliation with the club, he worked in every department, with full years dedicated solely to golf course monitoring, housekeeping, and maintenance, respectively. He views this apprenticeship experience as a fundamental phase in his life in which he absorbed the wisdom and knowledge of those who had come before him. Recognizing that many young people today are not cognizant of this tremendous opportunity to grow through learning from their predecessors, he would advise the next generation to adopt such practices.

Taking the time to learn a business from the bottom up in this fashion also equips a leader with the valuable ability to empathize with employees, as Todd's situation demonstrates. Maintaining a sincere respect and appreciation for his staff is an important facet of his management philosophy, and it seems that the success of his approach stems from the brand of deep compassion that can only be achieved by having stood in his employees' shoes in the past. Embracing the old adage to treat others as you would wish to be treated, he strives to maintain a hands-off management approach to give staff members the opportunity to carry out his vision in their own way. When an employee demonstrates hard work and commitment, his praise is sincere, personalized, and specific, underscoring the individual's effort in detail.

By instilling this quality of sincerity in his relationships with both club members and staff, Todd was able to transcend historical barriers between the two that had, in the past, posed them as adversaries. At the club's Seventy-Fifth Anniversary, he promised to break down the walls between management and membership to create a unified and cohesive front. With this revolution in climate and attitude, board meetings are no longer sites of conflict. Rather, management and membership are working together to decide what is best for Kenwood as a whole, fostering an atmosphere that is more conducive to innovation and progress than ever before.

Considering his remarkable ability to promote unity within his club and within the families of his community, it comes as a surprise that this great strength also manifests itself as Todd's greatest challenge—a struggle to separate work life from family life. On one level, Todd's situation is not unique from that of many other Americans with resource-intensive jobs that demand a considerable amount of time and energy. Like so many of us, he makes a conscious effort to "draw the line" at the end of the workday, liberating himself from frustrations and tensions so that he arrives home happy and ready to greet his wife and children.

On another level, however, Todd faces very individual struggles as a family business owner, in which the "line" between the work sphere and family sphere is often blurred and difficult to define. Working intimately with a family member in business can at once serve as one's greatest motivation and one's greatest insecurity, for only those close to our hearts could inspire such perpetual examination of self and practice. In his own experience, Todd utilized the assistance of a personal business coach specializing in family dynamics as a mediator and mentor. While many family businesses fail due to the internal pressures they face, the Chamberlins were able to channel their experience into a creative force that has advanced both their familial ties and their enterprise as a whole.

Reflecting back upon the hallmarks that define Kenwood, the two themes of calculation and risk repeatedly arise and complement one another. If a family business is risky, Todd moderates the stakes through employing the knowledge of an expert coach. If constructing a cutting-edge fitness facility was risky, it was offset by thorough research and analysis of the costs and benefits. It is this combination of calculation and risk that consumes Todd's days as president of Kenwood. He may no longer be sweating beneath the hot summer sun, but he maintains the same degree of focus and commitment that he had as the young lawn mower in his father's photograph. Gathering research, experience, and the opinions of members, staff, and specialists, he synthesizes these various pieces of information into comprehensive plans for the future that are ambitious yet plausible. His next brainchild, a project in the works, is the construction of a racket and paddleball facility. One skeptic asked him why he would want to do such a thing when no other club in the area has attempted it. In characteristic fashion, Todd replied, "That's exactly why.

Brad Chandler

The Clout of Common Sense

"That'll be twenty-five cents," said the young entrepreneur. The customer handed him a quarter, and Brad Chandler proudly passed over a Blow Pop in return. At age twelve, he had just turned a profit of twenty cents—four times the amount he paid for each lollipop when he bought them in bulk from the local drugstore. "I had eighty bucks in change at some point and thought I was rich," Brad laughs now. He likely developed the idea of reselling the lollipops at recess from observing his father, an attorney who had always been self-employed. "At an early age, I came to understand that with money, you can buy stuff—toys, radios, cassettes."

While life has gotten considerably more complicated since the time of his Blow Pop vending, the same entrepreneurial spirit shining through Brad's childhood ingenuity still permeates his character today. As the President and CEO of Express Companies, he approaches business with a very similar mindset and attitude—except nowadays, he deals with houses instead of lollipops.

Express Homebuyers, which is housed under the Express Companies name, was founded in late 2003 and excels at the purchase, renovation, and reselling of properties from distressed sellers, shepherding approximately 200 houses per year. This turnaround figure is especially notable in light of the fact that a typical home needs $50 to 55 thousand in repairs and takes approximately six months to complete and resell. The majority of distressed sellers today happen to be banks, but this was not always the case. In the past, clients most often were individuals who were facing foreclosure, divorce, bankruptcy, or job loss. Others may have been faced with repair costs that exceeded their means, or who simply felt a lack of interest to work with a realtor.

Along this line, Express Companies also houses Express Realty Services, a full-service realty company launched in April of 2008. This year alone, they are estimated to engage in about eight hundred transactions totaling over $100 million in sales, distinguishing them as the fastest growing realty company on record. Considering the vast success of this venture, Brad hopes to add other enterprises to the Express Company name in the future to supplement their current efforts, extending into realms such as lending and construction.

The business-savvy mentality that warranted so much profitability, both in the lollipop industry of the 1980s and in the housing market of today, stems from Brad's ability to consider and wield perhaps the most powerful tool a person can boast—common sense. A vital contribution of this common sense approach to Express Companies has been the development of systems and documentation, allowing a company to standardize its processes and services and then to streamline employee turnover by minimizing the need for active training when hiring and delegating. The true impact of this common sense approach also seeps into his leadership philosophy, which focuses on empowering rather than disciplining. Oriented around the core values of candor, speed, innovation, and accountability, his employees are motivated by the fact that they work to support an enterprise of integrity and inspiration. Brad achieves this through a management style that is oriented much more around what he can do to make his employees satisfied rather than what they should be doing to keep him satisfied—a unique yet effective perspective. "If you've got a good employee, make sure they're happy," he advises. "Err on the side of going above and beyond for them."

In reviewing these pivotal aspects of success, one would be fascinated to learn that so many of the techniques Brad employs today are not the product of formal schooling. "It's amazing how much they didn't teach us in business school," he remarks. "The only differences between you now and you in five years are the people you meet and the books you read," he continues, quoting a popular adage. In fact, he learned many of the most powerful aspects of leadership and business management not in the classroom, but through books. In ninth grade, he came across the book *How to Buy Real Estate with No Money Down* by Bob Allen. Enraptured by the idea of unlimited earnings potential, he pursued a degree in Residential Property Management at Virginia Tech with a concentration in Real Estate. He had worked hard to achieve his real estate license promptly upon graduation and went to work for a small property management firm in Waynesboro, Virginia. As the youngest property manager, he helped turn around distressed property and stockpiled the experience that would later bring so much success with Express Companies. Then, after receiving his MBA from Wisconsin University, he assumed employment with a developer who bought run-down apartments, fixed them up, and sold them as condominiums.

Though Brad reflects on this time as an excellent tutorial in corporate American culture, he knew he wanted something more from his professional life but couldn't quite put his finger on it. Then, in late 2002, his neighbor's house was purchased by an investor that Brad happened to chat with one day. The man explained how he purchased houses below market price, fixed them up, and then resold them—a novel concept that Brad had never even thought possible. "I made up my mind that that was what I was going to do," he reflects. Partnering with Jud Allen, a colleague with similar entrepreneurial goals, the concept of Express Companies first came into existence. "Every month that went by, I got more persistent. I saw more investors and knew that if they could do it, I could do it," he says.

After months of determination, Brad received a call from a woman living in a three-bedroom house with five or six kids who had failed to pay her mortgage. He had spoken with her several months before and had made an offer, but to no avail. Now, however, the house was to be auctioned the following week, and she had nowhere else to turn. "I understand you're an expert at this," she said over the phone. "Can you buy my house?" Bereft of funding, his mother loaned him $20,000 for the transaction. Under the tutelage of the gentleman who had first introduced him to the business, Brad then succeeded in buying and reselling the house, generating a profit of $43,000 on that single property alone. Not only was his hard work paying off monetarily, but he had improved his client's quality of life as well. "She was able to move her family to a much nicer, newer house that she rented out West," Brad reminisces. "She had told me that their only other option had been homelessness. She absolutely loved me." After the initial purchase of this property in July of 2003, he purchased five more by September, and the early stages of Express Companies' success had begun.

Among the most compelling aspects of the business's development to date is their initiation of professionalism into an industry that traditionally operates with a more mom-and-pop style mindset. While many of his competitors hide behind 800 numbers and refrain from even offering a physical business address, Brad has always aimed to build a culture of openness, honesty, and systematic reliability. Perhaps it is for this reason that Express Realty Services has risen to the number one team in Keller Williams out of 76,000 agents in North America.

Another vital piece to Brad's success puzzle is the utilization of systems building that his strong commitment to common sense led him to pursue. "We've been about systems since day one," he explains. Developing set processes and procedures has allowed them to dramatically improve upon one of the industry's major weak points: taking advantage of internet leads. Today, Brad reports, only two percent of internet leads are responded to in the home buying and real estate industries. Recognizing this vulnerability, Express Companies maintains a call center that is staffed seven days a week, ten hours per day, with aims to become a 24/7 operation. Calls are answered immediately, and an in-house lender is on hand to assist with any caller who is not pre-approved. "We have really upped our level of service," Brad confirms. In fact, Express Realty Services was first fashioned to capitalize upon the leads generated by Express Homebuyers, exemplifying Brad's innovative approach of identifying and filling the holes that have prevented similar companies from achieving success.

In addition to its strong systems focus, Express Companies was also founded with an indelible passion for marketing. In the early days of Express Homebuyers, Brad was working a full-time job and parenting a newborn son but still found time to sit at his kitchen table to hand-address hundreds of envelopes advertising his services. The company's current task force, comprised of a marketing director with thirty years of experience supplemented by three support personnel, two marketing coordinators, and a social media expert, utilizes a wide array of venues to broadcast their message. While their bread and butter over the years has been TV advertising, they also boast an incredible internet presence which Brad has been cultivating since the company's inception. Additionally, Express Companies is currently preparing to launch an aggressive radio campaign that will be supplemented with a thorough direct mail campaign, emphasizing a marketing strategy that is both eclectic and comprehensive. "It's one of the things that makes us so unique, and has been a big factor in our rising success," Brad confirms.

With this success in mind, Brad's vision for the immediate future is crystal clear: to become the first agent team to ever sell a billion dollars worth of real estate in one year. "We chose not to participate in the recession," he explains, in mock nonchalance. While the words are said in jest, the incredible reality at their core cannot be denied. Brad has steered the tremendous growth and success of Express Companies amidst a terrible economic climate and through one of the worst real estate markets history has ever seen. At the rate things have been going, he believes this goal can be achieved within five years. If, however, he succeeds in developing some of the strategic partnerships currently in the works, that annual sales figure could double.

The incremental yet rapid growth chronicled in these goals is structured to achieve Brad's ultimate goal for the company, which is nothing short of universal acclaim. "I would hope my professional legacy to be that Express Companies becomes one of the most admired and respected real estate companies in the world," he says. Young entrepreneurs should be especially encouraged by the grandiose quality of his vision considering the humble beginning from which it stems—common sense. When combined with quality coaching and an unwavering will to succeed in your passion, one can expect the kind of triumphs out of life that Brad's story so inspires.

Cindy Clare

The Lifelong Learner

It's hard to believe that Cindy Clare, president of Kettler Management, has never had to look for a job in her life. An international relations major at the University of Virginia, she had always planned to go into the foreign services but found herself temping at Charles E. Smith shortly after graduating, learning the ropes at one of the leading commercial real estate companies in Washington, DC. After a month of temping, Cindy accepted an offer of full-time employment and immersed herself fully in the industry, taking classes and absorbing valuable insight into the business's nuance. Within three years she was promoted to Regional Property Manager, and she had worked her way up to senior regional manager within ten. In 1995, she left Charles E. Smith for the Mark Winkler Company to run their residential division and then, in 2005, accepted an offer from Kettler Management to serve as senior vice president. Within three months, she was promoted to president of Kettler, exemplifying the kind of career ladder ascension that most only dream of accomplishing.

It would be wrong to assume, however, that the road to success was always paved in gold for Cindy. The eldest of four children in a military family, she babysat for extra money from age twelve. She worked for Hechinger's, a Home Depot-esque chain, as a cashier and customer service representative on nights and weekends, and she was employed part-time for the athletic department during her college years. She had always possessed a willingness to work hard and to do whatever needed to be done, which translated well to her experience in the real estate industry. This can-do attitude, combined with her genuine patience and interest, allowed her to go from a recently graduated temp worker to president of one of the top-ranked housing developers in the nation.

At its founding in the 1977, Kettler Management focused primarily on home development work. As it evolved over the years, it took on land development and tax credit apartment development dimensions. Then, in 1980, it evolved further to include a management component that eventually undertook both conventional and affordable housing projects. This diversification of the development and third-party management aspects of the company is perhaps the major turning point in Kettler's history, transforming its business model and allowing it to offer ongoing supervisory expertise in addition to property building.

In an industry fraught with uncertainty and risk, the road Cindy took to achieve her current position is among her greatest fortes. With personal experience at virtually every level of the business, she has positioned herself as an expert and offers unparalleled insight—a trait that has proven invaluable in navigating the rough waters of real estate of late. As Cindy explains, the markets have decreased business in the development sector while systematically increasing the demand for third-party management. She understands the real estate market as cyclical, posing the idea that management is ever more important when development is down because the rational owner aims to get as much as possible from their existing properties. These are the challenges that put Cindy's experience to the test, and with the healthy growth stemming from her influence, it is clear that she delivers.

Kettler has enjoyed tremendous expansion under Cindy's leadership, expanding from 8,000 units to 13,000 units in DC, Maryland, Virginia, and New Jersey in the five years she has headed the company. Kettler is truly unique in that it manages a full range of assets that span from affordable to high-end luxury, and Cindy attributes much of its success to this scope. She also believes that their prosperity stems from their innovative web-based marketing techniques, with their well-designed website supplemented with profiles on popular networking sites such as Facebook and LinkedIn. Whereas most companies refrain from utilizing technology-based marketing for affordable units, Kettler's progressive vision fully endorses this practice, and their success speaks for itself.

The accomplishments of any company, however, can only be measured by the success and drive of its individual employees. Drawing upon her own experience in the workforce, Cindy strives to equip each staff member with all the tools necessary for accomplishment. She aims to provide career paths similar to the one she, herself, had access to, opting to promote from within whenever possible. For Cindy, success is living, breathing, and organic; it lives within the people of Kettler Management. A team builder at heart, her style of encouraging and developing people is among her greatest strengths and has allowed her to get where she is today.

With such an emphasis on people skills, one would hardly believe that Cindy was, in her own words, painfully shy as a child. She typically met friends through her younger siblings and hated to be put in situations in which she didn't know anyone—a stark contrast to her current extroverted demeanor. As she matured and found that her responsibilities demanded strong customer service skills and connections with others, she rose to the challenge, realizing that burdensome tasks become easier the more you work at them. Thus, through careful attention and strength of will, she was able to transform a personal challenge into one of the greatest assets in her professional repertoire.

In addition to serving as a testament on overcoming fears, Cindy's story is a how-to guide when one isn't quite sure what-to. For the individual who knew from an early age what they wanted to do in life and stuck to it, direction is hardly an issue. But for the vast majority of us without such pointed premonition, deciding what to do with our lives can sometimes be daunting to the point of paralysis. According to Cindy, however, you can never know what direction your professional life will take until you actually get out into the field and start working. Maintaining a flexibility of spirit and optimism of heart allows one the openness to seize opportunities as they arise. As Cindy explains, she never intended to become the president of a company. Rather, she always sought to challenge herself and to perfect her craft. Success lies not only in consistency and reliability, but also in pushing the envelope and making a difference, always asking yourself what you can do and learn to evolve yourself and your pursuits.

Though she has reached what is generally thought of as "the top," Cindy does not stop asking the very same questions that got her there in the first place. In managing the overall operation of Kettler, she is continually building relationships, working with clients, pitching new business ideas, and strategizing for growth while maintaining the quality and integrity of the company that have become so integral to its reputation. In addition to promoting her own professional development, it is now her job to spur and inspire peak performance in the people and properties of Kettler Management. With her proven passion for challenge, learning, and advancement, it seems the road of life could not have led her to a better place.

Amidst these pressures, Cindy approaches the balance between work and personal life with a calm and matter-of-factness that is characteristic of her but surprising nonetheless. As the president of a fast-paced and growing company and also the mother of a teenage son, one would imagine a sizeable obstacle in managing work and family life. However, Cindy portrays a firm grasp on her responsibilities as both a leader and a mother and how those responsibilities interplay in her life. Her son, who she describes as her greatest success, is already an active member of society, participating avidly in school and sporting events. She understands that she cannot make it to every event, but if she puts one on her calendar, her staff understands the plans to be non-negotiable. Considering that women are still in the minority in senior leadership, Cindy's example is an inspiring one for anybody hoping to serve in such a demanding position while also raising a family. As the member of a group of several women executives pledged to advise and support one another, she demonstrates that, while sexism is still an issue in the workplace, women have the power to promote opportunities both for themselves and for each other.

Without a doubt, the interconnected relationships, partnerships, and support systems that Cindy facilitates create a web of mutual promotion and teaching that are the hallmark of her impact in both her professional and personal lives. As an instructor for the Institute of Real Estate Management, she claims that she learns just as much from her students as she hopes they learn from her. Always open to examining knowledge from different angles, she is a firm believer that every experience in life, whether positive or negative, has a lesson. By seeking and embracing these lessons, one can always expect that the next step taken in life will be forward, whether you're just starting out or an established veteran on the lookout for the Next Big Thing.

Tony Coombs

The Mission-Driven Mind

For many business owners, entrepreneurship is solely about the product and the profit. But for Tony Coombs—founder, president, and CEO of TCoombs and Associates, LLC—it's about something more. His motivation far surpasses the confines of his office space, extending beyond each of his 800 employees and the countless clients for whom he does business. It's more than a means of making a living; it is a means of making a difference.

Indeed, while TCA is known for its excellence in telecommunication, security, and healthcare logistics services, the primary driving force behind Tony's ambition is his ability to transform society through the initiation of positive change. His business accomplishes this by providing opportunities to individuals who might not otherwise have them. In an effort to instill vision in populations that are oftentimes marginalized, Tony's professional pursuits demonstrate that personal ideals and social change can have a place of worth and prominence in the world of business if we allow them to.

Tony moved to the U.S. in early adolescence but was born in Jamaica, a country stricken with considerable poverty and scant privilege. After moving around New York City, his family settled in the Bronx, where his father worked as a janitor and his mother served as a maid, cook, and nanny. With his parents each working multiple jobs, Tony found himself compelled to keep order amongst his siblings, ensuring that they did their homework after school and stayed out of trouble. He views this early experience as his first brush with leadership, as well as an early exhibition of the three traits that laid the foundation for his success: discipline, faith, and focus. Growing up in an environment where respect was highly valued, he inevitably developed strong skills in patience and restraint. His parents, who he refers to as the most influential people in his life, laid in him a foundation of honesty and self-control, and he has thoroughly assimilated these traits into his character over the years.

Though Tony received an athletic scholarship to attend NYU after completing high school, he instead enlisted in the marines per his father's direction. The year was 1977, with the Vietnam War winding down and a thick tension looming in both the political and social climates. Training on a base in rural South Carolina, Tony faced several tiers of prejudice—one for being a black man, and another for being city-raised amidst the perception that strong character was cultivated through country work. Navigating with an immutable sense of self, however, Tony was able to endure the preconception and was later deployed throughout the Pacific. He served for twelve years and excelled at his position, recalling that the patience and discipline he had fashioned in himself as a child gave him a tremendous advantage.

After finishing active duty, Tony took up residence in Florida and married the woman who would later prove herself an integral pillar of support in his success. After obtaining an engineering degree, he organized a janitorial business with six or seven employees, predominantly family members, while he applied for jobs at IBM. The rag-tag company afforded the young family a reasonably comfortable livelihood and gave Tony the opportunity to learn business management skills until his persistence paid off and he received a call from IBM in 1985 offering employment at their manufacturing plant. He was then transferred up to the DC metropolitan area in 1986 and found the work fulfilling for the following decade. During this time, however, he couldn't help but observe his wife Shanda's work in the social services. Seeing so many low-income individuals whose lives could be transformed through opportunity and vision equipped Tony with the impulse to build a vehicle that could fulfill those needs.

It was this impulse that hovered in the background of his thoughts when he stepped away from IBM and sought to start TSystems Group in 1999, which would later evolve into TCA. The business didn't earn a profit until 2003, adding stress at that time when the family was attempting to put its two eldest children through college. They were subsisting on Shanda's salary while Tony spent the majority of his time marketing himself, doing cabling for different department stores and finally coaxing business from the government of Maryland to provide service in county high schools. He positioned himself as a specialist in telecommunications, with services including cabling, wiring, and phone systems. Through his experience at IBM, however, he knew that success would be limited until he diversified his company's repertoire.

The timing could not have been more opportune when he attended a conference in the summer of 2003 and met a retired lieutenant colonel, Roger D. Stull, who had since established a cyber security company. The two joined forces, expanding the portfolio of TCA to include CNA, risk assessment, and Information Assurance services. Diversification was even further achieved through partnering with another air force retiree, John Olson. Between the three veterans, the company now boasted a strong working knowledge of the staffing and technology needs of both the air force and the Office on Disability. As a result, TCA's expertise spanned telecommunication, cyber security, and healthcare. Today, its service list correlates to these three main divisions but is even broader, encompassing engineering, technology, security, healthcare services and staffing, financial services, human capital management, telecom and access control, development and construction, alternative energy solutions, and TCA Foods. Diversification paved the road for the success and longevity that Tony predicted, and the company grew to $90 million in revenue in less than a decade. The incredible growth even won TCA a spot in Inc. Magazine's list of the top 500 fastest-growing private American companies in 2007.

In addition to its strong business model and its ability to deliver quality, budget-friendly, and timely services to its clientele, one of TCA's greatest fortes is its company culture. With an employee retention rate of nearly 100%, Tony says that TCA is defined by this culture—one that is not so much delineated by the amenities of working at TCA (like the gym and racquetball courts on the tenth floor of their home office building), but rather by the permeating sense of community that Tony strives to instill. He builds this ethos by serving as a leader that his employees can reach out to whenever they need. Despite his many responsibilities, he is adamant about being "in the trenches" both professionally and personally. "Nobody is an employee or a number," he remarks. "Everyone who supports what I'm trying to do is an extension of my family."

Tony's commitment to his "extended family" is further confirmed by the fact that TCA assumes between 50 and 80 percent of its employees' healthcare costs. This may seem impossible in today's economic depression, but Tony accomplishes it through a simple adjustment of profit margin. His overall attitude and business model fuel unparalleled employee morale and loyalty, which in turn engenders a workforce that is committed, focused, and impassioned, whether local or at one of TCA's international sites.

Young entrepreneurs entering the workforce today could benefit greatly by modeling themselves after Tony's level-headed approach to leadership. He reflects that his best business decisions were when he chose to stay the course, have faith, and not panic. In making these choices, he advises to stay attuned to your gut instincts while also emphasizing the significance of context. "Under no condition would I make a decision solely based on a dollar amount," he emphasizes. While cost-effectiveness should not be discounted, one must always stay true to oneself, choosing a course that maintains the integrity of your mission and vision.

Perhaps it is exactly this coherence between professional success and personal objectives that drives Tony's success. Contrary to many business owners, he is rarely stressed in his work and does not draw a clear distinction between the professional and personal spheres of his life. In this sense, it is as if he is working every minute of everyday, whether physically, mentally, or spiritually. Because his company's culture is so in harmony with his personal values, working imparts energy rather than depleting it.

Tony is currently using this self-sustained energy to look toward the future of TCA, which will hopefully entail evolution both in service model and in mission breadth. In terms of the business's portfolio, he hopes to build up the commercial aspect so that it is more in balance with the company's federal contracts, which now comprise approximately 90% of its focus. He has also developed an exit strategy that extends the chain of command to his eldest daughter and first employee, and ultimately to his two granddaughters. Considering this, combined with the fact that over 70 percent of TCA's employees are female, the company's present and future echo Tony's firm commitment to the respect and promotion of women professionals. "I believe the world would be a better place with ladies at the helm," he explains.

In terms of mission, Tony also hopes to take the vision behind his organization to the next level by focusing more on advocacy. As a private company committed to providing transformative opportunities to low-income yet talented individuals, TCA provides an effective and lucrative business model that succeeds in instigating positive social change as well. Tony's next step is to bring political awareness to this model in the hopes that other businesses can observe and adopt such principles, enacting change on both local and global scales.

These big picture goals may seem grandiose, but Tony takes each morning to reaffirm their clarity in his mind and strives to deliver this visualization to his staff as often as possible, keeping the team focused and driven. A respectful and fastidious observer, he has honed his relational skills such that he can tailor his communication style to best correlate with his audience—a proficiency that allows for effective exchange regardless of demographic variance. Whether in the trenches or in the conference room, whether at work or at home, and whether in street clothes or a suit, Tony's unity of personal and professional purpose is at once refreshing, transparent, and powerful. It is one that has generated swift and sturdy success thus far, and one that promises to impart solidarity and growth in years to come.

Michael Croxson

Faith in Human Goodness

As a pioneer in the for-profit credit counseling industry, Michael Croxson's business philosophy is perpetually optimistic and forward-thinking. "What do I want to do next?" and "What needs to be done?" are the axial questions he continually asks himself as he works to streamline the process of debt-relief. His work focuses on how to best align these two questions so that they can be answered with clarity, like an image that gains substance and detail as the distance between a person and their goal disappears.

While Mike has many responsibilities as the President of CareOne Services Inc. and the COO of the Ascend One Corporation, his most fundamental function is that of "culture police." Aside from his roles as the operator of CareOne's sales, a contributor and leader in public policy and community relations decisions, and as part of founder Bernie Dancel's executive team, Mike's primary efforts remain focused on making sure his company maintains the same energy and concentration that first attracted him many years ago. But, in order to understand Mike's value system and talent for value recognition, one must first understand the company which he works to preserve.

Ascend One was founded by Mr. Dancel after a personal experience exposed him to the need for a service which, at that point, did not exist. In his early twenties, he went through a difficult divorce and, though he had always identified himself as financially astute, found that this unexpected change in his life had wrought similarly unexpected financial consequences. After exhausting all of his options, Bernie didn't know where to turn for help and was advised to meet with a traditional credit counseling associate. When he called to make an appointment, it was scheduled for a date two weeks in the future. When he arrived at the meeting, he was informed he was not in possession of the correct documents, and his meeting was delayed another two weeks. These wasted weeks were crippling, and Bernie was forced to declare personal bankruptcy per the advice of an attorney.

Credit counseling began as a service in the 1950s, but had remained stagnant as a business paradigm until the early 1990s. After his unsatisfactory experience, Bernie committed himself to finding a way for people who are struggling to know that there is a resource immediately available to them—a resource that would reach out to them by means that were regarded as unconventional at the time. He started a company that introduced the use of phone and fax to its business model, foreshadowing the focus on technology that would lead to so much success throughout its evolution. The organization grew to 300,000 customers within four years, making it the largest in the industry. However, in 1997, Bernie decided that in order to best serve those affected by crises similar to his own, he must step away from the traditionally non-profit credit counseling model and become a for-profit technology, processing and consulting company that would serve the entire credit counseling industry. *This* is the company—Ascend One—that Mike Croxson joined in 1999. The Ascend One family of businesses currently includes Amerix, which advises credit counseling agencies on back office and technological strategy, and CareOne, which provides consumers with a host of solutions and education for debt management issues.

Though Mike thrives in his current position, he could not have predicted his future career path when he first graduated from the University of Virginia back in 1986. His initial plan was to work for several years after his graduation and then to go back to school. He received multiple offers from New York banks and banking entities and planned on taking a position with Morgan Stanley, but before doing so he accepted a dinner invitation from the head of Human Resources at First Union Bank, Sid Tate. Mike's interests were more directed to human resources, and Mr. Tate offered to create an associate program for him that would allow him to work in HR at their Charlotte office. This offer had special implications for Mike, since his family lived in Charlotte as well, so he embraced it.

Fully immersed in his new role, Mike found himself a profound interest in the behavior of those around him. This innate ability to observe can be traced back to Mike's parents, who were both behavioral scientists at heart. His mother worked as a clinical social worker, school counselor, and eventually as the manager of all the counselors throughout a school system, constantly exploring what makes people "tick." Mike's father, in turn, served as an Episcopal priest and was an excellent role model for Mike.

"I saw my father at the forefront of instituting change in society," Mike explains. "My parents focused on doing things the right way, and for the right reasons." During the Vietnam War, his father was a pioneer in the unification of dissentious citizens at his church. It was the first time people of different races, sexes, and demographics had lived together, seeking shelter at the church in commandeered

Sunday school rooms. His father taught him that there is no reason to limit the meaning and impact of any given opportunity, claiming that an individual should be welcomed in his church regardless of their political views. During such a politically charged time, this was truly progressive thinking. Correspondingly, Mike's mother imbued him with extreme optimism, especially as it related to people. She taught him to focus on what was "right" about an individual's perspective instead of what was wrong, pointing out that each perspective has something valuable to offer. Today, Mike finds himself employing these lessons constantly in the workplace and in business settings, asking those around him to describe their thought process in great detail and nuance.

The bilateral nature of Mike's philosophy that later compelled him to team up with Mr. Dancel was informed by a seminal experience in his youth when, as a college junior, he served on the board for a single-sex boarding school in Lynchburg, Virginia. Mike's father had served on this board before his passing, and so Mike was asked to serve on in his stead. The school had recently transitioned from a single-sex to a co-ed environment and was struggling to identify a path for the future. "How do you take everything the alumni loved about the school and use it as a springboard for the future?" was the question on everyone's mind. After being immersed in the tradition of the school as a head counselor and member of the Honor Committee, Mike worked ardently to help lead others through the difficulties that came with change, and although there were hard transitional times, the school came to flourish in its modernized form.

"At the end of the day, people's willingness to tolerate change is a function of their trust in you," Mike explains. This timeless advice, tested through his experience with the boarding school, is now paramount to CareOne's business premise. As he describes, "If we brand ourselves directly to our consumer to portray what we bring to them as unique, and if we continue to deliver on that brand, then when that consumer is out of debt, they will recognize that we were in the foxhole with them and brought them to the brink of being debt-free.'" Mike reasons that this loyalty will allow CareOne to evolve one step further by developing services to help newly-debt-free consumers decide what comes next for them. "Whether it is retirement, or financing a college education, we will tell them how to get there," he explains. CareOne's goal, then, is to never give a client away, even after their debt has been eliminated. It also hopes to maintain the CareOne brand through innovative services like third-party deliverables. Although the financial supermarket concept is yet to be properly executed, Mike believes that CareOne has a unique opportunity to realize this dream since their customers come to them in times of great need. He also notes CareOne's exceptional reputation in an industry known largely for an overwhelming proportion of "bad guys." Whereas other companies aren't known for customer concern, CareOne focuses exclusively on the needs of the consumer and what is most important for them without conflict of interest or hidden agenda.

This philosophy, which serves as the foundation for all that the Ascend One Corporation hopes to accomplish in the future, is precisely the culture that Mike strives to maintain and promote on a daily basis. It is a culture centered on the conviction that human beings are fundamentally good at heart, and that the human spirit will persevere when given the right tools. "Financial troubles are rarely the fault of the consumer," Mike explains. "More times than not, the consumer that comes to us has incredible ingenuity and has figured out how to juggle an incredible number of balls before something unforeseen happens and knocks all the balls out of their hands, leaving them without an idea of which ball to pick up first." In helping individuals piece their lives back together to form solid futures, Mike's work enables him to make these ingenious people feel like valuable members of the community again. Always open to new thoughts, always interested in new perspectives, and ever able to see the good in people, his work ensures that the corporation remains true to its original values even as it expands toward new horizons.

Bernie Dancel

Remapping the Realm of Possibility

When Bernie Dancel divorced at age 23, he considered his options. He had only completed one year of college at the University of Delaware and had spent some time in the military in the hopes that he could pay for his remaining schooling while supporting a young family. With the burdens and bills from his marriage and separation adding considerable girth to the already pressing expenses of daily living, he quickly found himself amidst mounting debt and dwindling hope. When he sought the advice of an attorney, he was told that filing for bankruptcy was his only option. Though his financial liability slate was wiped clean, filing for bankruptcy left personal and emotional afflictions that persisted, casting a troublesome shadow upon his sense of self-worth.

The professional path that he pursued in the wake of these trying times is a testament to a conviction Bernie had felt in his soul all along—that people are inherently good, knowing the difference between right and wrong and generally striving to do what's right. With his feet back on the ground, he began a career in financial services, achieving lucrative positions as he learned how to assess investments and manage excess cash flow. The more he learned, however, the more he yearned to transition into a role that would help people who were struggling financially instead of those with excess. He dreamed of helping people who were more like the figures of his childhood—people who were trying to persevere amidst imperfect circumstances. The youngest of two boys raised by a single mother who worked odd jobs for restaurants, farms, and canneries, his passion for struggling demographics rested close to home. Thus, he leapt headfirst into the credit counseling business in 1992.

At that time, the credit counseling industry was stiflingly homogenized. All the organizations were nonprofit entities funded in large part by creditors, which created a conflict of interest that left much to be desired. The services were only revealed to consumers sporadically and usually not until a creditor had attempted debt collection and failed. Furthermore, Bernie felt as though the industry's leadership consistently missed the big picture because they had never been consumers of the services themselves, oblivious of the kind of financial stress they sought to assuage. After several months of industry exposure, Bernie couldn't take it anymore. But, rather than jumping ship and pursuing a less frustrating career path, he took a decidedly different approach: transforming the industry altogether.

Funded through his new wife's line of credit, he opened a shop with just himself and a phone. In the next five years, the one-man show evolved into Genus Credit Management and quickly became the largest nonprofit credit counseling agency in the country, earning over $100 million in revenue and instigating industry-wide change. The company owes its success in large part to its consumer-centric approach—a revolutionary shift from the previous model that was managed, controlled, and governed by the credit-granting community. Contrary to traditional protocol, they advertised and marketed their services readily. These advertisements used very specific and direct messages so people knew if they were qualified to call and had the option to seek help regardless of the depth of trouble they were in. Striving to eliminate common barriers, Bernie instituted a call center so people didn't have to take time off work and weren't forced to suffer the social stigma of walking into a credit counseling office. If a consumer was up at 2 AM worrying about how they might make ends meet, Genus Credit Management would be there to answer their call.

Perhaps the most inspiring aspect of this story is the fact that Bernie and his team were never acutely aware of their success, even as it mounted. As he reports, "We didn't know we were the largest at the time because we just had our blinders on. How do we help more people? How, how, how?" The company was continually streamlining their processes, improving their training, and exploring different channels of communication to spread the word. While delivering real and concrete help to consumers used to take six to eight weeks, Genus Credit had whittled the process down to forty-five minutes. Leveraging technology and building strong, informed relationships with creditors allowed Bernie to act as a responsible, compassionate, and positive mediator between creditor and consumer.

With Genus Credit Management growing as fast as the rest of the industry combined, Bernie took it upon himself to get out in the field and talk face-to-face with top creditors, banks, and collections departments. He hoped to acquire a more nuanced understanding of the players in his business so that he might better serve both them and their debtors. After this venture he resolved to transition away from Genus Credit, leaving it as a nonprofit in the hands of the management team he had put in place, and to launch Amerix Corporation in 1997. Through this new endeavor he aimed to advise credit counseling agencies, teaching them a new business model and providing the technology they would need for implementation. By assimilating these core competencies into the industry, he was able to reach more consumers and instigate even more widespread change than before.

And yet, it was not enough for Bernie and his corporation to affect change in the industry alone. When he next set his sights on establishing a for-profit credit counseling agency, he found that many states had difficult barriers in place for that kind of business. Instead of throwing in the towel, he set about changing legislation state-by-state, building an environment in which he could operate objectively and without conflicts of interest. Thus, CareOne Services Inc. was established and affiliated with Amerix under the Ascend One Corporation family. 3Ci, a business designed to market the CareOne brand, was also formed under Ascend One. Today, CareOne offers credit counseling while also partnering with other professionals to provide access to resources on bankruptcy and debt settlement. It maintains a unique flexibility, able to thoroughly examine the consumer's needs to make recommendations that are truly in the best interest of a person in need. Instead of taking the traditional one-size-fits-all approach, they run individual analyses on their customers. In this sense, it is truly more than the sum of the services it provides, taking a holistic approach and providing the consumer with options. Their results are truly a testament to this approach, with a significant percentage of clients able to pay back the entire sum of their debt.

One other riveting aspect of Bernie's business model is his utilization of the consumers themselves as resources. Because credit counseling and debt management relies so heavily upon behavioral modification throughout the plan's implementation, advice and support is especially critical. Consequently, Bernie's company facilitates communities of consumers who can come together and share tips and stories. "We turn to our customers as the experts because they've been doing this," Bernie explains. "They come up with solutions because they're forced to or else they won't be able to make it through the month." Not only does this provide a valuable support structure for the consumer, but it eliminates the traditional expert vs. debtor dichotomy that was so prevalent in the industry before Bernie's influence. Whereas credit counselors would oftentimes talk down to consumers in the past and do further damage to their self-concept, the consumer is now positioned as a respected and valuable perspective in the credit counseling process.

This unbridled willingness to collaborate is a key ingredient to Bernie's success as an entrepreneur, allowing him to assemble answers from many diverse sources into coherent and comprehensive solutions. "I don't need to have all the answers myself," he says. "I know there are answers out there and I'll look anywhere it takes to find them." Relying on the input of his executive team, his management style hinges upon collaboration and, above all, upon trust. "They trust each other completely," he says of his team members. "Whatever it is they're doing, it's for the greater good of the organization. This allows them to have important disputes and great discussions."

The passion at work behind Ascend One's leadership is undeniable, providing a firm foundation for the organization as it continues to revolutionize and redefine the credit counseling industry. It is staggering to think that the passion fueling their continued growth and success today is the very same passion that was present at the humble kitchen table all those years ago where Bernie first began his crusade. It continues to fuel his conviction in the face of certain discouragement, giving him the persistence to keep asking questions until every answer is found.

Recalling many occasions where he was told his goals were impossible, he advises future generations with the kind of optimism one can have faith in. "Believe you can do anything you want to do," he urges. "Mistakes are lessons. Successes are even more lessons. Failure doesn't bother me. I believe in where I'm trying to go so much that it's real." His greatest piece of advice to young entrepreneurs is to find this same passion within themselves—that wellspring of energy and excitement that brings happiness and contentment regardless of how profitable it is. Transform it into a career and use it to carry you through failures and setbacks, which there surely will be. "There's nothing that's impossible," he reminds us, living proof of the empowering words he speaks.

Matthew Dean

Designing Your Destiny

Throughout grade school, Matthew Dean had always excelled effortlessly at mathematics. One can thus imagine his surprise and horror when his ninth grade math teacher recommended him for the second best math class instead of the best. High school had raised the bar somewhat in terms of demand and standards, and the boy's diligence had not yet escalated along with it. Though the packs of football pencils given out as prizes for elementary school math competitions were a thing of the past, Matt found a brand new source of motivation—his own willpower, and his own destiny. Determined, he asked Mr. Burns what he could do to maintain his status in the highest class. "You must ace the second half of this school year," the teacher said. Matt rose to the challenge and excelled with flying colors, and true to his word, Mr. Burns changed his recommendation.

From this experience, Matt drew so much more than just a renewed drive for math, which carried him through to receive his master's degree in engineering later on. Beyond the specific skill, the challenge cemented in him something he had always known in his soul but hadn't actually firmed into a concrete guiding principle. "Nobody's going to give you anything or carry you. You've got to get out there and do it yourself," he confirms. Now the President of MARKON Inc, a government contracting and consulting company specializing in management solutions, Matt could not have gotten to where he is today without this revolutionizing conviction in personal agency.

MARKON is a spinoff of MKI Systems, which has since been purchased by L-3's Command & Control Systems and Software (C2S2) Division. Matt assumed employment at MKI, a full-service professional organization focusing in the needs of the Marine Corps, in 2005 to help diversify the company into the intelligence community market. He started his division as a one-man show which grew to nine team members by 2007 when L-3 decided to purchase the enterprise. The new ownership wasn't interested in an intelligence division, and Matt was not interested in the new ownership, so MARKON was born. When they first spun off, they specialized in providing consultant services to the intelligence community and were earning $1.2 million in revenues. Just a few short years later, they are now over forty employees strong and have amplified revenues to $7 million, fanning out across industries through the translatability of their knowledge base.

Being the professional services company that it is, MARKON essentially sells time and manpower to federal government organizations with the goal of improving functionality through the use of professional resources. The feature tool in this arsenal is project management, and MARKON's ability to capture key processes and replicate them across subjects has played a vital role in its success. "Our business model has been to serve across government agencies because our method is translatable," Matt explains. "The Army, Marine Corps, CIA, NSI,

DIA, DNI, etcetera—the same types of skills are valuable across all these markets."

MARKON's real value lies not in its method, however, but in its matter. "The motivation of our people to succeed is what truly makes us unique," Matt acknowledges. His team, which is monitored by seven managers, understands the intricacies and nuance of the business that allow them to play the game with unparalleled expertise and offer exceptional service while still balancing the business aspects of the work.

The fascinating thing about Matt's success is that it doesn't stem from outside influence, but rather from a strong internal locus of control that marked his comportment even at an early age. Throughout his youth, he doesn't remember being pushed or micromanaged when it came to academics or athletics. It was always expected that he and his three brothers should maintain good grades and attend college, but his parents, who divorced when he was ten, did not actively talk about the future. Matt's mother had chosen to focus on her family and her children instead of pursuing her career, and this fact serves as a strong source of motivation in his life and work today. "My mom chose not to take her career into her own hands as a sacrifice for us kids," he remarks. "If I don't take full advantage of the opportunities in my life, I'm wasting what she gave me."

Matt's first handful of jobs were acquired throughout his high school years and revolved around construction, most notably for Cates Electric. The manual labor was intensive, with one particular instance standing out in his mind in which he was required to dig holes and insert grounding rods for a major electrical system. His first rod took him eight hours of backbreaking labor to install due to the ground's impenetrable quality—a disheartening end product that only hinted at the effort required to obtain it. When he reported his single accomplishment to a coworker later that day, the man shrugged his shoulders knowingly. "Yes, you will work hard, but it never really amounts to anything," the laborer told Matt. This remark emblazoned into his mind a strong resolve to do well in college, taking pains to ensure that he set himself up for a professional journey instead of a professional dead-end.

After starting college at Virginia Tech, Matt acquired a job in database building assistance at the World Bank's Facilities Group. "I wore a shirt and tie to work for the first time," he remembers. "It was my first chance to experience a real office job." When he graduated in 1991 with an Industrial Engineering Degree, he found the job market somewhat barren. After a slew of interviews, he was finally offered a government position with the Department of the Navy as a program analyst in a cost analysis shop. In this capacity, he served to assist different Navy programs in mapping out current costs and predicting future expenses. This was essentially his entrance into the government acquisition and support world while also giving him first-hand training in the client service environment as he worked to develop relationships with different customers.

Though he would receive frequent accolades on his performance excellence, Matt was barred from promotion because he didn't have seniority, and he was turned off by the lack of control over one's own destiny that the atmosphere engendered. Not only had he reached the kind of dead end he had vowed to avoid, but his personal learning and evolution had come to a standstill. "I realized I wasn't going to be gaining any additional skills after the first five years, and I didn't like the resigned attitude that the system is the system," he recalls. "Realistically, I knew I couldn't change the system, so my only option was to take my career into my own hands."

With that, he left to enter the Big Six management consulting world through employment at KPMG Consulting, which became BearingPoint in 2002. Throughout his nine years of employment there, Matt served as a management consultant in a wide variety of industries. The experience allowed him to see how many skills can be translated to different markets and environments, honing his insight for his later leadership with MARKON. BearingPoint's decrescendo commenced in the early 2000's with its transition from a partnership model to a public company model. Aware of the writing on the wall, Matt left for MKI Systems in 2005 before BearingPoint's collapse and eventual merger with Deloitte Consulting.

Despite its impressive evolution and diversification, MARKON's story is far from complete. "We're still a new company and haven't finished setting the foundation yet," Matt says. True to his upbringing, which focused on a general striving for accomplishment rather than a specific micromanaged path toward success, he remarks, "I don't feel like I have to hit a certain figure in revenue to accomplish a given goal. Rather, I just focus on making good, smart decisions." Not only does this approach lead to reasoned judgments and solid returns, but it heightens team morale by instilling sound confidence within MARKON's employees.

Now, as the company's past performance record and reference list grows, Matt and his team are working on building the company's accounting system and overhead infrastructure as they begin to aim their targets on bigger fish. "The sky's the limit," Matt says lightheartedly. "I'm particularly excited because it gives opportunities to our employees to expand their skills, almost as if they're running mini MARKONs themselves." This mindset showcases the leadership philosophy that drives the enterprise—one of interconnected fates and genuine interest in the success of others. "It's all about the team approach," Matt explains. "I truly believe that the best way for me to be more successful is for my employees to enjoy this success as well."

In advising others along this quest for collective success, Matt urges the kind of openness and awareness that has kept him in perpetual evolution over the years, both personally and professionally. His method echoes what seems to be a current trend in American society toward life-long personal skill strengthening and diversification. "I remember reading an article that explained how, for generations, people thought it was risky to change jobs," Matt recalls. "But now, at least in our industry, staying in the same job allows your skills to get stale." So, where his role was once in contracts, security, finance, business development, and recruiting, he has incrementally yet steadily shape-shifted into the strategist and broad-scale leader he serves as today.

It is safe to assume, then, that the future of Matt's role as President of MARKON is far from set or static. In this light, he also emphasizes the crucial part that long-term planning and vision plays in success. "The big thing I've learned recently is that I'm in this for the long haul, and my decisions are reflecting this realization," Matt remarks. "Investment in training, going out of our way to hire good people, getting into new markets even though they may not make money this year—all these are an automatic yes for me now. Maximizing my 2010 income would be at the expense of my 2015 income, so I'm not going to do that," he explains.

Inherent in this recipe success, however, is a certain fascination and will of character. "Be a sponge. Soak up everything," Matt insists. It's how we keep life fresh. It's how we stave off stagnation, keeping the self on a perpetual journey toward betterment. And it's how we put our future back in our own hands, molding something truly remarkable and unique from the raw material of status quo.

Patrick Dean

Imparting a Vision

Most children revel in Saturday mornings as a time of unparalleled sloth, characterized by sleeping in late and watching cartoons in bathrobes and slippers. Patrick Dean, however, knew that he could count on quite the opposite. From the time he was fourteen, he knew his father would be pulling the sheets off his bed come Saturday morning, waking him to come work at the family factory. Seeing his own father work hard and enjoy the benefits, Pat soon saw how hard work enabled him to transform the visions in his head into reality, like finally being able to purchase the green Schwinn bike he had been eyeing for a long time. Now the President and CEO of Associated Builders and Contractors (ABC), Pat will never forget the days when he learned the value of a dollar and, perhaps more importantly, the value of a vision.

After developing a solid work ethic modeled after his father and completing only one year of community college, Pat left for California when he turned eighteen to pursue his love of golf. He enrolled at Fullerton College and worked as a busboy at a nice restaurant, waiting tables and golfing in his free time. After actually working on a golf course for a while, one of his customers suggested he go work for a produce market. With little to lose, he decided to take the man's advice and was promoted to night shift manager at the largest produce warehouse in Los Angeles within three months. As a twenty-two year old kid, Pat was making an impressive living until the warehouse was forced to close due to union pressures.

The young man was then promptly picked up by National Sanitary Supply, a company dealing with building maintenance materials and chemicals. "I did quite well there, but I wanted to do better," Pat reports. It is for this reason that he accepted an invitation to enter the development business in real estate, where he worked for two years before suffering a bad business deal that cemented his disenchantment with California. "Everyone was mortgaged on the hill," he remembers. "Everyone was divorced and broke but driving BMWs." He packed up, moved home, and then did concrete work for a month in Chicago until a friend finally convinced him to pursue an opportunity with ABC.

ABC is a nationwide construction trade association that has focused on commercial industrial contractors since its inception in 1974. Pat began working with ABC in 1985 selling memberships to the association's Chicago chapter. Among his wisest investments was a cell phone installed in his car—a very new and innovative technology at the time. "I would come into the office in the morning, find out where I was slated to go that day, and then take off through the Chicago suburbs, operating business through my car phone," he reflects fondly. Salesmanship came naturally to him, having grown up with a father who used to serve as District Regional Manager for Encyclopedia Britannica and who would take him along for sales calls at the age of seven.

Two years later, Pat relocated with ABC to Portland to learn more about the business aspects of the association and then became President there. He served in this capacity for two years before he was recruited by the national organization to assist with chapter and employee development throughout the country.

The excitement and constant coming and going inherent in the position was a good fit for Pat for three years, but once he married, he decided that the extensive travel associated with the position wasn't conducive to starting a family. "In my eyes, the risk and reward wasn't great," he laughs now. It was around this time, when he had just begun considering other options, that the opportunity to become President and CEO fortuitously came his way. Thus, he accepted the position in 1992, marking a tremendous turning point for the association and for himself. He now heads the Virginia chapter, which is comprised of three offices throughout the commonwealth.

"To be honest, the association was pretty decimated when I took over, so I really couldn't do anything but look good by comparison," Pat jokes now. The chapter had been built on local politics, and with the devastating economic climate, membership had faced a drastic decline. Patrick Dean, however, had a vision. "My greatest gift was sales, and I explained to them how we could sell ourselves out of the mess we were in," he describes. "Maybe they were weary from trying to keep the association afloat, or maybe they really did believe in my excitement and confidence." Indeed, if the association leadership had been looking for a savior, they came to the right guy.

"To win over existing leadership and transform membership recruitment when you're starting off with nothing, you have to be able to paint a pretty compelling picture of what the membership's values *will* be," Pat explains. "You must have a vision and a way to communicate it such that people can see where you're taking the group and what the long-term benefits will be." His ability to impart such charisma and incur such trust was lent tremendous conviction from his prior experience as a salesman, which breeds not only an exceptionally thick skin, but also a strong-willed nature that remains impervious to external negativity. "As a salesman, you've heard *no* so many times in your life, so what's one more?" he points out.

By transforming the association's entire structure and placing a prime focus on education, training, political advocacy, informational services, and community service, Pat was able to take an organization that was 170 members weak and $100 thousand in debt and completely transform its attitude and feel. As a result, ABC went from $400 thousand in revenues in 1992 to $3.5 million in 2009. Their membership base has followed a similar trajectory, now hovering at around 650 with aims to escalate to 1,000 in the next five years.

"Our substantial success and growth can be attributed in large part to good membership, strong leadership, a committed team, and an exceptional staff," Pat explains. Such tremendous progress would also not be possible without his decision to shift the association's focus to education. "At my first planning meeting as President and CEO, I said we would make ourselves the leader in construction trade education in the Commonwealth of Virginia," Pat remembers. "We accomplished this, and we remain so today."

Being an education leader in the industry means a full range of different programs that include training in craft and apprenticeship, general management, leadership and development, and safety. Theoretically, the association treats the concept of membership as a product whose worth is thus strengthened through the addition of education, providing training at considerably reduced costs such that a member's return on investment is highly attractive.

This is not to say that things have always run smoothly for Pat and his tenure at ABC thus far. The early years did not fail to test his capacity as a leader when he was faced with the sprouting of other construction trade groups that threatened to further fragment an already splintered industry. More recently, as well, he has been challenged by the struggling economy to keep membership up and operational costs low. As the failure of similar associations suggests, overcoming these obstacles could not have been accomplished without his nuanced experience supplemented by his empowering leadership philosophy and capacity to both attract and retain quality team members. Through retaining several key individuals while also hiring a host of new employees with the capacity to support his vision while contributing vital expertise in fields like communications and politics, ABC now boasts 13 full time staff members and 50 part-time instructors.

The leadership style Pat employs to manage his employees is not modeled after a single person or one ideology, but is rather a patchwork quilt of observation and character traits picked up throughout his life experience. "You watch people and see different skills throughout your career, and maybe you don't see the whole package in one person, but instead you find different pieces in different people," he reflects. The philosophy he's assembled over the years is thus one of inspiration rather than fear. As long as customer service remains the top consideration of ABC staff, Pat veers away from micromanagement and encourages his staff to take risks and make mistakes within reason as they pursue the goals he lays before them.

The most compelling aspect of his leadership style, however, remains the ability to impart a clear, honest, compelling vision of the future, thereby lending those around him a new nearness to the objectives at hand. "Being able to use the art of storytelling paint a picture of what the possibilities are is key," he explains. "Beyond this, I would urge one to keep in mind that patience is certainly a vital component to leading a successful life, but impatience can sometimes create positive outcomes as well," says Pat, as he advises young entrepreneurs entering the workforce today. To this effect, impatience can be a powerful motivating factor that pushes one to reject the status quo in favor of progressive change if the status quo falls short of one's true vision.

Furthermore, Pat implores young people to work hard at getting a solid education and meeting as many people as possible in one's areas of interest in order to create the most accurate conceptualization of reality possible. This consideration is particularly important when it comes to painting the kind of vision Pat so excels at, lending this picture a credibility and soundness that only empowers and expands it impact.

Lori DiCesare

The Power of Risk

"There are two different types of people," explains Lori DiCesare. "There are those that plan their entire future and want to know the end result before they get there, and there are those that don't think about the end result, just taking each day as it comes and knowing the end result will happen. This is what I do." Though she admits this can sometimes be a curse, it is also among her greatest attributes. It is the trait in her that, she believes, has made her life's path so different from many of her peers. It's the trait that allows her to embrace the exhilaration and free-fall of risk, and the trait that gave her the courage to first start her own business. Now the President and CEO of Legal Placements, Inc., a staffing agency specializing in legal staffing throughout the country, Lori hasn't thought twice about her leap into the abyss.

With a Masters in teaching and a specialty in learning disabled and emotionally disturbed children, she never imagined that she'd one day found a legal placement firm. However, after working as a paralegal to help fund her higher education, she found the field both challenging and rewarding and recommitted her professional roadmap. Lori then worked as a paralegal for eight years, eventually realizing that law school wasn't for her but still aiming to remain in the legal field. Believing her next step was a position as Paralegal Coordinator, she sought out a placement agency that could connect her with the right law firm. The agency, however, readily identified her experience and skill set as ideal for a position in the legal staffing industry rather than a law firm. Though initially resistant to the idea, Lori decided to try it out and found that she loved the work. "Just as with everything, the key was finding the right agency," she explains.

Lori worked at a wide variety of agencies over the following six years, learning more about both the industry and herself with each new experience. She gained a more nuanced understanding of what she would and would not tolerate in a work environment, always maintaining a steadfast fidelity to her integrity and standards. "My father would always say that you've got to live at your job, and if there's something you vehemently disagree with, get up and leave," she remembers. "Always leave with grace and never burn a bridge, but leave all the same." Throughout her five-year employment with her last agency, she noted things she would do differently if she were in charge. Then, one day, she resigned her position and found herself launching her own business the next. Guided by legal council, she saw to it that the transition was honest and lawful.

With only $5,000 in savings and no credit lines to fund the venture, Legal Placements got off to a tenuous start. With two young children to support, living was tight for the first six months while she refrained from paying herself. Lori had no business plan, taking things in stride. "Honestly I never thought about the next day," she admits. "I had to only think about *that* day. No book would have taught me what I needed to know. I made mistakes and learned from them. It's been quite a ride."

Though her first months as a business owner were not easy, Lori wasn't alone. When friends would learn of her vision, they were eager to lend a helping hand any way they could. Whether it was stuffing envelopes or providing free accounting services, Lori was inspired by their optimism and support. She also drew constant strength from her father's unwavering faith and confidence in her. Legal Placements was profitable six months after its inception, and it took a year for the company to replace Lori's income. Because of her ample experience working with and for attorneys, conversing with them and dealing with managing partners, she was able to offer a seasoned and knowledgeable product that was soon in high demand.

Reflecting back on the tremendous risk involved in Lori's decision to break out and found her own company, many wonder how she had the courage to do it. The key to her success primarily extends back to her willingness to risk. "There are people who could go out and do what I've done, but they just aren't risk takers for whatever reason," she explains. Another crucial ingredient to her success was the fact that she had essentially built a client base before she embarked on her mission, as ninety percent of her business at the previous agency came with her once she departed. This reality echoes the third primary ingredient of her triumph, which was her experience and expertise. To Lori, success is not about worrying what the future may or may not hold, nor about trying to micromanage the aspects of life that are beyond one's control. Rather, it's about truly knowing one's product and committing to it 100 percent.

Today, Legal Placements matches opportunities for contract and direct hire attorneys, paralegals, legal secretaries, and IT professionals. Contract and direct hire attorneys supply their biggest source of revenue, especially during massive bouts of litigation such as the recent incidents with Toyota and BP. With fourteen in-house employees and 250 to 300 contractors out at any given time, its impact extends far and wide. While its three offices are located in DC, Northern Virginia, and New York City, they staff projects nationwide.

The staying power of Legal Placements stems in large part from Lori's strong work ethic, which extends back to her early years. Though it may have been bred out of necessity considering that her family was of modest means, she quickly recognized its value and has aimed to cultivate it throughout her life. "In that sense, I feel very privileged that I didn't grow up in an affluent family," she explains. Her parents were very strong and influential figures in her life, working hard to make ends meet and putting Lori and her brothers through parochial school. From the age of sixteen, she sought jobs lifeguarding, working in the deli department at Wal-Mart, and wherever else she could find them. Having to support herself through college and graduate school further stretched this work ethic. At one point, for example, she was managing three jobs simultaneously just to pay for everything. "I lived on peas out of a can for a year, but that's okay," she laughs now.

Perhaps the greatest source of strength fueling this work ethic was the voice of her father, who had always told her with earnest conviction that she could do anything she put her mind to. The eternal optimist, he always gave her the impression that there were no boundaries to what one could accomplish. "Never forget where you came from, and always be honest. If you run your business with these two thoughts in mind, you'll be fine," he would tell her. He also taught her to stick up for herself and not to feel inferior in the presence of someone who held a higher degree than her. "At the end of the day, it's what did *you* do in your job? What did *you* accomplish? Did you do the best you could?" he would remind her.

It is this sense of honor, focus, and tenacity that Lori strives to instill in her own children today, and that she looks for in both her employees and contract employees. With this in mind, she encourages young entrepreneurs to start at the bottom and work their way up in much the same way that she learned and mastered an industry before starting her business. "I don't have patience for people who don't work hard," she states. In this sense, the recession has been a particularly interesting time for Legal Placements. The staffing industry was hit particularly hard due to lack of hiring, and she remembers that it was a wake-up call to everyone. In making difficult layoff decisions, work ethic was among the primary determining factors for her. One of her top producers would say, "This is not a time to complain; this is a time to buckle up and get back to work." It is this attitude that will bring professional success and staying power, she advises.

Despite her demonstrated commitment to hard work, Lori maintains a sense of genuine fraternity throughout Legal Placements. "My employees are my friends," she says. "They've been very loyal to me, and vice versa. We have great days, but we also argue the way a family does. Everyone has their moments, but you work through it." This is perhaps an echo of her upbringing, which was rich with Italian heritage and the closeness of family. "When I was brought up, there were never enough chairs at the kitchen table," she reminisces. "Dinners would last forever, and everyone was welcome to join in." Now, with a degree of that same closeness infused in her work atmosphere and in her relationships with clients, her agency emanates a genuine care and commitment to the well being of its employees, its contractors, and its clients.

So what comes next for Legal Placements, and for Lori? The terrain of the staffing industry is in continual flux, with new rules and regulations being added to the mix. Positioning her firm at the forefront of this evolutionary process will continue to hold a seminal place in her plans. "Everything is a lot more complex," she concedes, "but that's the fun of it—the challenge, the result, the catch.“ She will also continue her unwavering focus on her other full-time job—being a mother. "Undoubtedly, my best decision has been my kids," she affirms. Lori will continue to nurture and teach them as she evolves her business and herself, ready to take the next big risk when it comes along.

Donna Evers

The Renaissance Touch

At first glance, one would assume Donna Evers is a writer and academic scholar. With a Masters in English, she is currently conducting a private study of Earnest Hemingway's life and works while continuing to act as an avid contributor to *Washington Life Magazine* and *The Georgetowner*. She has also begun to consider compiling her material into a book that will examine the history of Washington, D.C. from a unique angle.

On second thought, perhaps she is instead a historian by trade. She has, after all, given many talks on the subject of Washington history and continues to receive invitations to do so. In our attempts to label Ms. Evers, however, our efforts are further confounded by the fact that she and her husband own Twin Oaks Tavern Winery in Bluemont, Virginia, and have just recently begun to bottle and sell their own wine.

With proficiencies that span such a wide range of whimsical categories, augmented by the fact that she is also a painter who loves to spend time in the Paris apartment she shares with her husband, one would assume that Donna's career lies somewhere within the realm of right-brained partialities—a profession that is predominantly intuitive, artistic, and creative. How surprising, then, to discover that she is in fact the proud founder and owner of Evers & Co. Real Estate Inc., a group of eighty agents committed to excellence in the sale of real estate in the D.C. Metro area.

"Real estate pricing is not a science," says Donna of her industry. "You need all the input you can get to do it." In dealing with real people and their most intimate environment—the home—her inclinations in the more creative aspects of life set her boutique-style firm apart from its competition in ways that are as natural as they are compelling. As such, when Donna walks into a room, she doesn't just see a piece of property—she sees stories, history, art, and potential, which all contribute to her ability to match the right homes with the right people.

Evers & Co. was founded in 1985 in Chevy Chase, in Northwest Washington, D.C., and has remained an independent entity ever since. "Washington is a thinking person's city filled with people that truly reflect on their consumer choices," Donna observes. "There's a lot of competition in this region, but people here are not necessarily going to fall for a franchise name. They're very discerning and want to deal with someone who's going to be answerable to them." That's exactly the kind of accountability and innovation Donna has ingrained in her business, and its success reflects this effort. Accomplishing $310 million in sales last year, Evers and Co. is on track to increase that number in 2010.

Donna had been an agent for ten years prior to opening her company's doors, and her experience lent her sufficient ammunition to cope with the rollercoaster that ensued. Evers & Co. enjoyed the boom market that lasted from its inception until 1989, when a crash in 1990 heralded eight years of poor market conditions. The climate finally leveled out in 1998, allowing the company to gain ground and hit another peak in 2005. "We're very subject to business cycles, so we've got to be prepared for that," says Donna. Riding the waves and taking things as they came, she decided to grow the business in 2005—then a company of thirty-five agents. The expansion initiative wasn't implemented until 2006, when they opened a second office downtown. This became their third office in addition to their locations in Chevy Chase and Bluemont, Virginia, which had opened in 1988. "You have to watch what's going on in the industry and strategize for how you're going to maximize success through that," she reflects now.

Donna first became a real estate agent because of her natural affinity with houses, architecture, and renovations. After marrying in 1963, she and her husband began purchasing homes in great locations and fixing them up. To date, they have redone twenty-three properties, two of which are in Europe. The pair began renovating and reselling houses because they moved around so much when they were younger, so it worked out well that something she did for fun would sometimes turn out to be profitable as well.

As an agent, Donna felt as though her skills improved every year. An agent is, after all, an entrepreneur at heart, as they're required to grow their business and spread their own word. Taking these requirements, Donna used her own natural inclinations and skills to make a good career great. With an eye and ear for aesthetic charm, historical significance, and high quality, finding the right homes for the right clients was second nature for her. "Figuring out how to market a piece of property so it will sell is a creative challenge, and it's wonderful to be able to help people solve their problems with your skill and expertise," Donna explains. "It's what I liked most about being an agent."

Though her broad spectrum of interests is truly unique, she is far from alone in her creativity at Evers & Co. "The thing about truly creative people is that they aren't stingy with their ideas," she says. "They share freely because there's always more where that came from. Our agents are smart, creative, outgoing, and always out there learning new things." The company is thus a highly collaborative atmosphere, engaging in weekly pricing exercises in which people share a broad consensus of views on how to maximize the price and stability of a property. "We all help each other. We're like one big family," Donna says. "I've aimed to engender a great, friendly, cooperative atmosphere from day one."

This strong emphasis on community and creativity perhaps stems from her childhood growing up in Hermansville, Michigan, a close-knit town of only 530 people. "It was Earnest Hemingway country," she remembers. One of her schoolteachers set up a small one-room library in the basement of the community building where the town's basketball games were held, and she devoured books voraciously. At age ten, she moved to a town of two thousand, which seemed mammoth in comparison.

Donna received her undergraduate degree at the University of Michigan and then moved to California to teach school. While there, she met and married her husband, Bob, and pursued her Masters degree at the University of California at Irvine between the births of her first and second children. She then took an eight-year hiatus from her career while raising her young family but decided to get her real estate license after her third child, John, started first grade. After moving to the DC metro area, her husband was always very supportive of her career and business. In fact, they were always somewhat like accomplices in the process. He had done work in small business consulting while in California and worked for Gerald Ford followed by the Counsel for International Economic Policy after coming to Washington, but he was never too busy to maintain a lets-do-it attitude when it came to purchasing, renovating, and moving on.

With this perpetual, almost ritualistic flux, one might think that Donna would seek stability through having a long-term plan. Aside from having early revenue goals, however, she largely abstains from such practices. Instead, her philosophy is of a more reactive and immediate nature. "If you're always thinking and always looking, you will know what to do when the time comes to make a big change," she explains. Her spontaneous personality compels her to seize opportunities when she sees them, which stands in considerable contrast to the nature of her husband, who is more mathematical and systematic in his planning. Though she values his opinion, she generally sticks to her own philosophies in running Evers & Co. "I make decisions very quickly, but I take into account how people will react before I do so. I don't mess around," she says, reflecting on her consensus style of management.

If Donna were to advise a young entrepreneur today, her most urgent instruction would be to take action. "Figure out what you want to do and go do it, for heaven's sakes!" she says. "People waste their whole lives worrying that it might rain tomorrow and they don't do all the things they might want to do." According to Donna, planning ahead is almost detrimental in the fact that one can start to worry about all the things that might go wrong instead of embracing the momentum of the present. "You really can't worry about it, just do it!" she emphasizes. It is precisely this attitude that has allowed Donna to pursue such a vast array of interests, attaining excellence in a variety of fields and using her well-rounded nature to inform her work.

When considering herself in the context of contemporary society, however, Donna sees herself as a departure from the norm. "This is not a time for Renaissance people," she comments somewhat wistfully. "This is a time where people respect specialization, when one person can do a particular thing that nobody else can do. I am not that." A better conceptualization, rather, is that she is not *only* that. As a woman business owner poised at the helm of an extremely successful real estate firm serving the nation's capital and surrounding areas, she has certainly mastered one thing with a firm hand. What makes Donna's story so compelling is that she made the time to embrace other aspects of life as well, viewing the world not as a compartmentalized building but as an open plain. She dared to be a Renaissance woman in an age where such specimens are growing few and far between, and the choice has enriched both her business and her life, building an expertise in her industry that is all her own and leaving no room unexplored.

Joseph Gargiulo

Family Focus with a National Presence

When the folks of Goshen, New York, had a question about hardware, they knew they could trust the young boy working at the local store to serve them with enthusiasm and savoir faire. Joseph Gargiulo had, after all, started working for his father at age seven, helping customers find what they were looking for and keeping the shelves of Goshen Hardware stocked and tidy. Over the years, he observed his father eagerly and absorbed valuable knowledge about everything from plumbing, to electrical work, to paint mixing, to customer service. Joe's father had gotten into the hardware industry to help support his Father-in-law's burgeoning family business, Stuart Dean—a building restoration and maintenance company founded by Joe's grandfather, Edward J. Degan. Now the executive vice president of Stuart Dean and the division president of the mid-Atlantic region, Joe still considers his time at the hardware store as his greatest education, using the service skills he learned as a boy to attain success today.

"Actually, I originally didn't want to work for Stuart Dean," Joe admits. When he graduated from Boston College in 1977 with a BS in Accounting and Marketing, he moved to Chicago and worked for several large enterprises that ultimately left him feeling unfulfilled and immaterial. His brother, John, headed up Stuart Dean's Chicago office at the time and approached him in 1980, posing what Joe refers to as "an offer I couldn't refuse." The young professional would have to work significantly longer hours at significantly reduced pay as a salesman, but there would be opportunity to have an immediate impact in his work. Realizing that Stuart Dean was a part of his very blood and heritage, Joe recognized the ambition stirring in his soul and accepted the offer. He excelled as a salesman and was promoted to sales manager in 1984. He directed his small sales crew until 1986, when he was offered the opportunity to open a new office in either Dallas, Texas, or Washington, DC. "DC was a sleepy town, and real estate hadn't been discovered yet," Joe remembers. Submitting his proposal for the DC Metro Area location proved to be the best decision he ever made. With its respectable and stable rates, DC has since advanced as one of the most desirable real estate markets in the world, and Joe's office is now the largest and most successful division of the company.

In many ways, Joe's personal history resembles a microcosm of the family company's overall evolution to date. Just as it can sometimes take a single idea to change the course of a lifetime, it can take a single idea to transform an industry. Yet, as Joe's grandfather demonstrated, this may not be the first idea that comes along. In fact, it took six failed business attempts within a span of ten years before Edward Degan finally founded Stuart Dean in New York City in 1932. The fledgling company served as the sole distributor and applicator of Dupont Synthetic, the first clear synthetic lacquer coating designed to prevent architectural metals—specifically brass—from oxidizing. Later realizing the value in the product, the Dupont Corporation approached Edward in 1934 asking to buy the exclusivity rights. Ed, however, readily signed over the rights without accepting compensation, an act of integrity that would later reward him in spades when the lacquer became a war good during World War II. Though it was taken off the market during that time and distributed solely to the military for use on brass casement shells, a drum of lacquer would appear on Stuart Dean's doorstep each month, ultimately enabling the company to stay in operation.

When Ed passed away in 1954, Joe's four uncles—Gene, Gerry, Jack, and George—assumed leadership of the company and tested the waters of expansion by opening new offices in LA in 1963 and Chicago in 1969. Another dimension of service offerings was added as well, and as is the case with so many businesses, diversification spelled big returns for Stuart Dean. Until the 1960s, they had focused solely on metal refinishing, building a reputation of excellence through mastery of a narrow specialty. They noted, however, that the buildings they worked on had marble floors and walls. Thus, evolving into architectural stone maintenance and restoration was a natural progression for Stuart Dean. They became the largest provider of architectural stone maintenance throughout the next thirty years, concentrating in granite, marble, terrazzo, and exterior limestone. Then, in the 1990s, architectural wood was added to the repertoire, as well as architectural glass and the curtain systems used to protect building exteriors. With a service portfolio that provides comprehensive attention to the various finishes of a building's interior and exterior, clients can now rely on Stuart Dean to cover all aspects of a project without having to coordinate multiple contractors.

As time passes, Stuart Dean has also aimed to operate less like a family business and more like a corporation. Though all forty-plus of its stockholders remain family members and all but two of its CEOs have been within the family, it has expanded to approximately 650 employees worldwide and retains three (out of nine) non-family board members from outside industries. Joe recognizes the value of outside leadership and remains committed to incorporating it. The company culture prohibits a sense of entitlement, and decisions are always made in the best interest of the company as a whole. Consequently, Stuart Dean strikes a unique and highly appealing balance. They have successfully taken the personality of a mom-and-pop style small business and translated it to a national scale. With offices in the top twenty real estate markets in North America, they are equipped to offer on-site and personalized service to large clients nationwide. While Joe hopes to establish more uniform procedures to render their services consistent across offices, their national presence remains a great credit to Stuart Dean's staying power.

Joe's division, then, is perhaps the quintessence of this staying power. The Mid-Atlantic office is currently about eighty-five employees strong and does approximately $10 million in revenue annually. Joe remains active in the day-to-day operations of the office and also oversees the operations of the Florida office, which has about thirty employees. "This is what I do best," he says, referring to his current daily duties. In addition to fulfilling the various roles of financial overseer, personnel manager, and policy collaborator, Joe is still out in the field on a regular basis, making sales and monitoring on-site progress to ensure that the company's vision and quality assurance are maintained. When asked why he hasn't become CEO yet, he cites his aptitude and preference for the small business mentality and the close relationships it allows him to develop with employees and clients. Recognizing the importance of his brother John as a mentor and role model, he uses his own relationships with staff as opportunities to pass on wisdom and guidance in a similar fashion, exhibiting sincere interest in the lives and careers of his employees.

In developing these mentoring relationships and dispensing advice to young entrepreneurs just entering the workforce, Joe focuses more on character development tips rather than employment instruction. "Don't be too concerned about getting the perfect job, because the chances of you staying in that profession are miniscule," he counsels. His words are sure to assuage the fears of anyone entering the job market during these sub-optimal economic conditions. The focal point at such a juncture should instead be the cultivation of one's moral character and relational skills. "You must deal with people properly and ethically no matter what industry you enter," says Joe. Learn how to deal with difficult individuals by disarming them with kindness, and practice treating others how you would wish to be treated. This advice fits hand-in-hand with what Joe reports as his greatest professional challenge, which is personnel management. He indicates that it's hard to find individuals who are driven to do the right thing regardless of short-term interest. Young entrepreneurs who exhibit this strength of character are thus highly sought-after and will enjoy more success than they would otherwise.

Strength of character is even so important as to overshadow more traditional measure of intelligence in some cases. "My number one management philosophy is hiring good, smart, hardworking people," Joe explains. "I manage by feel more than numbers." Because the industry is so hands-on and relies heavily upon relational skills in addition to a strong knowledge base, he truly believes that effort can be the key ingredient to success. Even if one didn't get the top grades in school, there is a future for that person if the right effort is leveraged.

In reflecting back upon the road that led him here and in considering what the future holds for Stuart Dean, Joe's focus remains not on the success he has enjoyed but rather on the people and presences in his life that have influenced his career—and ultimately his life path—most profoundly. These are not grandiose figures of fame and history, but rather the common figures that occupy his everyday life. "I'm a faith-based person, so the Good Lord has taken good care of me," he says. He also speaks with a genteel and sincere warmth of his wife, older brother, and parents, recognizing that each has provided valuable skills and support. In a business that has flourished and expanded so far from its roots, its good to know that, for both Joe and Stuart Dean as a whole, the element of family continues to thrive as strongly as the company it created.

Jim Gibbons

Giving a Hand Up, Not a Hand Out

When Jim Gibbons graduated from Purdue University in 1985 with a degree in industrial engineering, he applied for jobs with 50 separate companies and, in turn, received 50 separate rejection letters. It wasn't that he had earned bad grades or had questionable records. The one thing working against him, it would seem, was his blindness.

Jim, however, was no stranger to the power of hard work and commitment. He didn't give up, and his persistence paid off when he landed a position with AT&T. Similarly, when he applied to Harvard Business School shortly thereafter and received another rejection letter, he persevered, applying again several years later and going on to become the first blind student to graduate from the school. Now, serving as the ninth President and CEO of Goodwill Industries International, Inc., Jim's quiet but adamant stance on achieving success in the face of adversity indicates an internal reservoir of resolution that never seems to leave him high and dry. "The ideas of leadership and impact were what motivated me then, and they're what motivate me now," he puts it simply.

It would be an understatement to simply say that Goodwill® has become a widespread and permanent fixture of American society. With 165 member agencies across the United States and Canada, and a global presence boasting more than 4,000 retail stores and donation centers across 13 countries, the brand is instantly recognizable and a common household name. An equally prominent aspect of the organization is the fact that its mission and impact extend far beyond the collection and resale of used goods.

In fact, Goodwill placed more than 150,000 people in jobs last year through its relationships with approximately 100,000 employers across the country. "We leverage the infrastructure of a $2.5 billion business built on donated goods retail as a platform to provide solutions for transitional employment, training and first-time opportunity employment for people who have trouble gaining or maintaining employment," Jim explains. As a result, Goodwill served nearly 2 million people in a variety of job training and employment services programs last year alone.

The enterprising agenda of the organization doesn't stop there. It extends even further to supply funding for various social impact and training services within the communities where it operates. In fact, Goodwill currently has $600 million in contracts, half of which goes toward employing people with disabilities in federal grounds maintenance, food service, and document management, to name just a few of its employment options. Yet another $600 million is held with direct program services in mind.

Goodwill's success is the product of many years of trial and error, observation, and improvement. It was first established in 1902 when Rev. Dr. Edgar J. Helms, a Methodist minister, began collecting goods from the community to give to the poor immigrants in South Boston. He soon realized, however, that people didn't want to receive handouts—

they wanted to earn what they received. With this in mind, he collected donations in anticipation of the first Goodwill store. The immigrants would also fix any broken items for sale and earned wages in the process.

The unification of this initial store and Helms' recognition of the value of a hand up, not a handout, spelled the birth of Goodwill Industries®. Soon, "the Goodwill way" spread like a systematic wildfire, as Helms went from town to town to share the idea, eventually taking the approach abroad as he traveled the globe. Helms was a compelling motivator and continued to rally support through the end of his life, acting as a strong advocate and speaker for the cause even after he resigned from the position of CEO in the 1930s. With that, the Goodwill we know today had begun to take shape.

This is not to say that the organization settled into a state of stagnancy thereafter. On the contrary, throughout the 1960s and 70s, it withstood a gradual transition away from being a faith-based enterprise as it began to hire professional managers instead of ministers to fill the roles of President and CEO at each local agency. Despite this shift, many people still consider the organization to maintain an element of the faith upon which it was originally built.

The various Goodwill agencies in the United States and Canada are referred to as *members*, and each has operational control over its stores, donation centers, contract services, and job training and employment services within their local communities. These members are essentially the lifeblood of the organization's ability to impart change. "Each member is structured to serve certain territories or regions," Jim explains. "This allows them an extraordinary synergy such that, when the organization has great projects or programs to implement, they can be replicated, scaled and launched as quickly as possible with local needs in mind." Goodwill Industries International, in turn, exists to provide leadership and service to the membership, but not to instill operating management directives in local Goodwill agencies. This business plan has allowed the idea to evolve from a movement to a social enterprise and to a scale such that power rests within local operations—addressing the unique needs of local communities and thereby making the greatest impact.

Perhaps the most compelling aspect of Goodwill is the simple elegance of its business model, which rests on the ability to connect several widespread dots across the planes of various social issues into the kind of constellation that lends a new breath of hope to each one. Take, for example, the 68 billion pounds of textiles that are sent to landfills each year. When someone donates a sellable item to Goodwill instead of adding to this waste, the positive impact extends both to the environment and to the community.

"We all have a responsibility to the communities where we live and work," Jim explains. "Goodwill had an opportunity to connect the dots in a meaningful way, so we did. As a direct result, we are an organization that goes beyond expectations, continually pushing ourselves to be truly great—today and for tomorrow. This is what I see in Goodwill."

As part of Goodwill's social responsibility efforts, the organization recently created the Donate Movement, a public awareness initiative focused on raising consumer awareness about the power of donated goods and how they impact both the environment and the community. The Donate Movement is envisioned to help Goodwill grow its mission and keep up with the increased demand for services by securing increased donated goods.

This attitude illustrates the strong platform of genuine, thoughtful and authentic corporate responsibility built into the company's culture that so profoundly distinguishes its market share and bottom line in a way that is not only ethical, but forward-thinking. "Consumers want to know that they're doing business with an organization that has a conscience," Jim points out. "All the data suggests that, even if this isn't the typical customer today, it *will* be the typical customer tomorrow. The new generation really feels strongly about this."

In many ways, Jim's life and experiences are a microcosm of the spirit of respect, responsibility, cooperation and supported independence for which Goodwill advocates. He grew up the youngest of eight children in Indianapolis, Indiana. His father, an engineer, was the quintessence of self-advocacy, hard work, and perseverance regardless of circumstances. It is very likely that, had such strong values been lacking in the young man's life, his diagnosis of macular degeneration when he was in the third grade would have had a crippling effect on him. Jim's parents took the news in stride, and resolved to maintain the same expectations of their son as they did for all their children. He was expected to do chores, to complete his homework, and to always treat others with respect and kindness. Despite this firmness, however, his parents never failed to provide him with the tools he needed to succeed in his endeavors. "I don't remember an evening when my dad wasn't helping me with my math homework, either reading the problems out loud to me or helping to explain the principles," he remembers.

"This blend of high expectations and constructive support figures strongly into my management philosophy today, as well as in the overall personality of Goodwill," Jim reports. In this way, high expectations are matched with a supportive culture and ample resources for personal growth and opportunity, creating the perfect climate for a strong sense of self-worth and prosperity to thrive. "When you have a clarity of purpose, goals and objectives, and then give your team the tools, skills and opportunities they need to garner their own independence, you create an impact as widespread and as positive as Goodwill's," Jim explains.

Throughout his childhood, Jim's parents always expected him to work hard and do good in the world, but they never anticipated that he would one day lead an enterprise as large and pervasive as Goodwill. "In truth, I always thought I'd spend my whole life in Indianapolis—that is, until I went to college and realized the importance of mobility," Jim explains. Starting his post-collegiate career in Cincinnati with AT&T and then transitioning to New Jersey, followed by a move to Boston for business school and an open horizon after that, he came to the conclusion that upward mobility was inextricably linked with geographic mobility. "Opportunity is the intersection of preparedness and luck, and it is mobility that imparts this luck," he explains.

Operating with this tenet in mind, Jim spent 13 years with AT&T and rose up the ranks until he was President and CEO of a $15 million, wholly owned subsidiary of the company. Later, he was offered the position of President and CEO with the National Industries for the Blind (NIB), a social enterprise focusing on employing people with visual impairments. "Working at NIB gave me the opportunity to step up, transitioning from an influencer to a direct player in terms of impacting the lives of people in need," Jim explains.

The position also facilitated tremendous personal growth, allowing him to use his skills in an enterprising way and on a larger scale while reporting to a Board of Directors. Jim spent 10 years in that capacity, growing the operation from $240 million in contracts revenue and $100 million in retail to $600 million and $300 million respectively. His transition to become the President and CEO of Goodwill Industries International in 2008, then, seemed like a natural trajectory for his impact to follow. "Goodwill is an incredible brand with a larger reach to help people with a broader range of disabilities and disadvantages. As such, I was presented with an opportunity to have a greater impact in an area that I'm very passionate about—the power of employment," he reports.

Now, it seems that Jim has arrived at the perfect intersection point—that place where meaning and passion blend with enterprise to build communities that are truly operate effectively. In short, it is a position that maximizes the impact he has always yearned to achieve. As such, Jim advises young individuals entering the workforce to target that spot where their skills and passions intersect in much the same way he did. He also stresses the importance of mentors—wise and experienced people from whom one seeks nothing but perspective. "When you can glean that perspective in a meaningful way and couple your skills and passions with an understanding that there must be a level of hard work in the equation as well, then you'll be able to launch your career in a very powerful way," says Jim. Such is the recipe to build the kind of experience, success and transformative impact that truly makes a difference.

BERNHARDT

WEALTH MANAGEMENT

Michael Gottlieb

The Personality behind the Practice

"Michael, I've talked with you more in the six months since I hired you than I spoke with my previous attorney in the ten years I knew him," remarked the client.

Initially, Michael Gottlieb wasn't sure whether to take this as a compliment or a concern, but his client quickly clarified. "I think it speaks to how comfortable I feel working with you," she said.

A partner at Apatoff Peters Ebersohl, LLC, Michael is markedly different from most lawyers, as his colleagues and clients often tell him. No, it's not the fact that he loves racing cars and has participated in the sport since law school, though the evolution of this particular hobby is a fascinating story all its own. Rather, it is the fact that most attorneys are primarily comfortable with the technical aspects of their work like drafting documents. While Michael excels in this expertise, he also brings something additional to the table—a personable, friendly, refreshingly human style of interaction that allows his clients to feel truly respected and heard.

"I feel like I can learn something from every client I have, and I *want* to," says Michael. He continues on to explain how understanding his relationship with clients can be likened to understanding the relationship between a driver and their racecar. "When the relationship works, you can go faster, accomplish more, and it's a heck of a lot more fun," he explains. Working with people to facilitate solutions that allow them to operate more efficiently is one area where Michael truly shines. "I love when people call just to run something past me," he laughs.

Apatoff Peters is a small, yet prominent law firm operating out of Rockville, Maryland, that was founded in 2005 by Adam Apatoff and Craig Peters. The two joined forces because they were dissatisfied with their experiences at their then current firms, hoping to launch a new firm that would serve the local business community with a new business model and a new verve for the industry. With Adam's background in technology and transactional work paired with Craig's expertise in tax, the firm has since blossomed from two to ten, attracting business through its reputation of providing downtown law firm services in exchange for a fair and reasonable fee. Today, the attorneys of Apatoff Peters generally serve as outside general counsel to clients that tend to be privately held companies, with several publicly traded entities seeking their services as well.

Excelling at the age-old strategy of dividing and conquering, each partner at the firm possesses a unique area of expertise that complements and strengthens its collective skill set. With focuses in corporate and business law, technology, transactional work, tax, estate planning, commercial real estate, nonprofits, commercial litigation, labor, employment, and both large and small businesses, they cover a wide breadth of specialties without sacrificing a foundation of comprehensive and in-depth specialty knowledge. Michael, for example, typically handles smaller clients ranging from startups to $20 million in revenue. His client base is markedly diverse, and the firm addresses each step in the entire life cycle of the clients' needs. "In this capacity, I'm the go-to person for my clients, whatever the legal issues are," he explains. "I handle or quarterback whatever comes up, whether its litigation, sophisticated transactional matters, etcetera. If a matter lies outside my realm of expertise, I have a wealth of resources in my colleagues to assist with addressing it."

Michael may seem to have found the ideal match in Apatoff Peters, but the road to the firm was anything but straightforward. After graduating from the Wake Forest University School of Law in 1997, he decided to pursue his interest in technology before commencing his practice of law and accepted a position as a programmer at Anderson Consulting. He left Anderson Consulting to accept a position with Arthur Andersen, where he assisted with a business concept aimed at helping large companies capitalize on their intellectual property assets. He was then ready to begin his legal career, so he finally began practicing law at a small firm in D.C., which broke apart shortly thereafter. He then spent five years employed at a different firm in Rockville. He was on a partner track there when he was recruited to another local firm, testing the waters to see what fit best with his personality and skill set.

When Michael interviewed at Apatoff Peters in 2009, the firm was confident that his success would grow very quickly if given the latitude to build his own practice—an opportunity they happily extended to him. "I decided it was worth the risk, so I went for it," Michael recalls.

At the time, he had been comfortable at his previous firm, making good money and considering investing in a business of some sort. He and his prospective business partner had considered an array of options, from a Laundromat to a check cashing business, but nothing had really spoken to them. "The idea of leaving my old firm was tremendously nerve-racking, but my wife provided great insight and advice by suggesting that if I was going to invest in any business, it should be my own law practice," he says. "Then, I realized that my 'happy place' wasn't about the firm, it was the type of work I was doing and who I was doing it for, i.e., my clients. Once I started representing local companies on a regular basis, I found that I loved what I did, and I love running into my clients around the community." Since accepting the position with Apatoff Peters and leveraging the new resources at his disposal, Michael's book of business has tripled. With the risk-reward paying off and the feeling of both finding and hitting his own unique stride, he considers himself extremely fortunate to have arrived at where he is today.

This deeply-rooted yearning to connect with people in a meaningful way perhaps stems from Michael's childhood, the terrain of which was largely defined by the six marriages and five divorces collectively claimed by his parents. As a result, Michael and his sister were raised primarily by a single working mom who didn't have time for an extensive social circle. "As I got older, however, I learned that the better you play with others, the more fun life is," he reflects now. "I never had a sense of community when I was younger, and achieving these types of bonds now is a strong driving force for me."

Michael's success stems not only from the fact that he thrives on fostering genuine and fruitful client relationships, but also from the simple reality that he excels at what he does. He is naturally skilled at identifying and predicting problem areas for his clients. "I tell my clients that my job is to do the worrying for them," he says. He accomplishes this insight through asking a series of related questions that hearken back to the Socratic method, aimed at unearthing true intent and hypothetical pitfalls. "I take a very personal interest in all of my clients' businesses so that when I'm negotiating for them, I truly take it on so I'm negotiating as if it's my own issue," he explains. "To this effect, I will push as hard as I can to get the very best result in whatever we're trying to do."

Michael's method of practicing law is also notable for his remarkable ability to build trust through following up. For example, he methodically contacts his clients with status reports even if there hasn't been any progress to note just to ensure that they know he's still thinking of them and that their particular matter hasn't slipped through the cracks. Managing his workflow in a manner that is as proactive as it is interactive thus allows Michael to build the kind of trust with his clients that enables him to be the best lawyer he can be. "The more trust my clients have in me, the better lawyer I can be for them," he describes. "It helps them feel comfortable being more open, which allows me to obtain that fifty-thousand foot view where I can see where they are, where they want to go, and how they can get there."

In advising young entrepreneurs entering the workforce today, Michael echoes the words of his own father, who urged him to find what he loved to do and pursue it because one should not spend thirty to forty years working each day and not enjoying it. "My father speaks from experience," Michael points out. "He didn't love his job, and he tells me how he would give up an awful lot of what he has now if he could have enjoyed the road more. So, find what you enjoy, work harder than everyone around you, and the rewards will come."

As for Michael, those rewards *have* come, both on the home front and at work. "I have a beautiful, bright, supportive wife who has given me a lot of flexibility to go out and build what I had hoped to build," he explains. He also has two wonderful children and has worked diligently to manage his time such that he can be an active and supportive husband and father while still accomplishing all he hopes to do professionally. "What's more, at work, I have a great firm environment with lots of fantastic people and fantastic resources," he adds. With these tools, he focuses on running his professional endeavor not only as a practice, but more so as a business.

In light of his achievements, many people would call Michael lucky, but he would caution against this terminology. "To some extent, every successful person has a degree of luck on their side, but luck comes from looking for ways and opportunities to become successful," he says, reminding each person that our destinies lay within our own hands to a large extent. "It comes from finding your own way into a position in which you can really accomplish things." As his wife, Sue, would say, it's a willingness to invest in one's self. It's the ability to know your own strength, whether it's promoting the personality behind your practice or something else altogether. It's taking the bricks of these strengths, applying courage and perseverance, and building something great.

Dawn Halfaker

The Persistent Patriot

When Dawn Halfaker first opened her eyes in the sterile hospital room, she was stunned. She let her shaken memory sift through what had transpired. A Captain in the United States Army, she had been deployed to Iraq five months before. Her platoon had been assigned to live and work in the city of Bacuba, where they had participated in raids, patrols, reconnaissance missions, forced protection, convoy escorts, and police training. One of her patrols had been ambushed, and a firefight ensued. When her vehicle was hit with a rocket-propelled grenade, the shrapnel had splintered through her right shoulder, and that's where the memories stopped. In her comatose state, she had not been awake to see the helicopter airlift her from the scene. She had been unconscious for the trip back to Washington, DC, and she had been unconscious during the amputation of her arm. When Dawn awoke in that hospital room, she knew her life would never be the same. She was twenty-four years old.

The road to recovery was not an easy one for Dawn, and her progress was further frustrated by the inevitable sense of denial that swept over her. Unable to see past her current condition, she would try to pretend it hadn't happened. The young woman suffered from a profound sorrow until one day, when her physical therapist led her down to a room where several soldiers were undergoing rehabilitation for their injuries. The first person she saw was a staff sergeant who had lost both his legs and had suffered severe facial burns. As the man wobbled hopefully on his new prosthetic legs, his wife and children chanted, "Go, daddy, go!" From that moment on, Dawn's perspective changed completely. "I learned that I was really lucky for what I had and shouldn't be dwelling on what I didn't have, and I got really focused on my future," she says.

Six years later, one would hardly imagine that the intelligent, poised, and successful young woman had ever had a moment of self-doubt. After the incident, she knew she wanted to maintain her strong military connection, especially the leadership aspects of her position. After attending several job interviews where nothing really clicked for her, she happened to meet an army colonel who had just started working with the Defense Advanced Research Projects Agency (DARPA) and needed a research program manager. He was looking for someone with recent combat experience who could envision the potential for research to save lives by leveraging technology on the battlefield.

Taken with this man's inspiration and passion to aid war fighters, she worked in a consultant capacity for him as she gained experience and developed a company of her own, which began to take form in January of 2006. Drawing on her unique skill set and nuanced knowledge of the national security community, she served on DARPA contracts investigating new strategies and materials that could be developed, commercialized and deployed to the armed forces to strengthen national security. She worked on these projects for two years while building Halfaker & Associates in the background and also attending Georgetown University at night to receive her Masters in International

Security. The U.S. had undergone "a very transformative era throughout the last decade," Dawn reports, "and I felt that I had unlimited potential to contribute in different areas."

As Dawn took on sub-contracts with DARPA, she hired people with similar backgrounds and experiences—namely veterans hoping to continue serving the mission who possessed valuable skill sets. In this way, Halfaker and Associates continued on a track of organic growth through the end of 2007, when it began winning larger contracts and adding critical mass to its staff. The company developed departments for human resources and finance, gaining a self-awareness that was strategic rather than tactical.

While Halfaker & Associates originally focused on national security policy, homeland security, and defense solutions business unit, it has since branched off into program management, consulting, PMO support, acquisitions support, IT solutions, and software development and integration. Though they have diversified their revenue streams, the majority of their business still comes from U.S. military contracts. It makes sense, then, that the company remains very mission-driven. In fact, the mission element of their service model accounts for much of their uniqueness as a company. "Personally, this company is a vehicle for affecting change in areas where I've been passionate," she says. "It is powerful that we can address an issue." From a business perspective, they have established themselves as a trusted partner to their clients through this mission-orientation, allowing them to invest in these clients both personally and professionally. Through sharing a common mission and vision with their clients, Halfaker & Associates is able to offer outstanding and highly-responsive service that tailors solutions to best fit the needs of each individual client. It is a partnership mindset and service model that larger companies cannot offer, allowing them to stand out amidst their competition.

Looking back at her business's evolution, Dawn points out that little things happen all along the way that cumulatively define the journey.

She can, however, put her finger on one notable turning point for the company—a time when it was enjoying success and growth, but without a means to advance to the "next level." As she reports, "developing a long-term strategic plan turned us into a *real* business overnight." When the fledgling group won a considerably hefty contract with the US Army Recruiting Command, they were forced to put infrastructure in place. In the end, they had over fifty employees on the contract, successfully supporting the mission and recruiting soldiers to enter the military. It was indisputable that Halfaker & Associates had come of age, truly developing into a notable force in its field.

Because Dawn embarked upon her professional journey at such young age, she relied upon the mentorship of several key individuals to make up for the business and consulting background that she lacked at the time Halfaker & Associates was started. "Sometimes it takes people looking in from the outside to see what the possibilities are," she remarks. She would advise a young entrepreneur to identify their mentors early on—individuals who have your best interest at heart and can answer the "dumb questions" to help you understand how to leverage what you have and what is possible. Now that the company has been operational for four years, she's looking inward at herself and how she can repay the favor by advising and mentoring others. Focusing her energies on wounded veterans transitioning out of the military, she now knows what questions to ask to help people identify their own unique paths in life.

Consequently, one other defining aspect of Halfaker & Associates that renders it so unique is the fact that it is a service-disabled veterans company, with over 70% of its employee-base comprised of veterans. More specifically, they are part of the Wounded Warrior Hiring Program, setting aside jobs for injured veterans and working to train, mentor, and develop those individuals to assume careers with the sense of purpose that so many of them lost when they left the service. "That was what was so hard for me," Dawn reflects, referring to the mission-orientation she lost when she was force to resign from the military. The company was a means for Dawn to regain her footing in a new life following her injury, and her efforts in turn now provide similar opportunities to people facing the same obstacles.

Dawn's current responsibilities at Halfaker & Associates include, first and foremost, the long-term success and strategic growth of the company. By laying out the path to success and honing the primary goals of the enterprise, she aims to set the gears in motion so that her employees can, in turn, act. She also identifies the responsibility she wields for the lives of others—a duty which she takes with the utmost seriousness. To Dawn, running a company is so much more than making sure the nuts and bolts are in place. More importantly, it is ensuring that her employees are receiving the tools they need to be successful and to reach their goals. Additionally, Dawn is constantly considering the company's role in the community. Through her service on the advisory boards of a number of nonprofit organizations, she extends the boundaries of both the company and of herself.

Reflecting back upon the past several years, Dawn is most proud of the team she's assembled. "They can do anything," she marvels, "and that is a powerful thing. Whether it's focusing on Wounded Warrior, or a charitable event, or getting a proposal out the door, they will get it done." To achieve this level of success, she warns young entrepreneurs against a mentality of finality. As people enter the workforce, they tend to believe that their entire lives will be locked into the first field they go into. This mindset is misleading and can often be paralyzing. "Just go for it," she advises. "Take risks. Take chances. This will eventually lead to the path that was meant for you." If one never goes out on a limb, one never discovers their talents, preferences, and passions. This process of self-discovery coupled with hard work and determination go hand-in-hand with Dawn's leadership philosophy, which is focused around constant learning and evolution. Not only does this involve the acquisition of wisdom and knowledge, but also learning about your teammates. "Whether it's a combat mission or a business mission, you must look to people," she says. "Treat them well, know them well, know their strengths, and know how to pull the best out of them." When it comes to passion for the mission, it is readily apparent that Dawn's enthusiasm and commitment are representative of her entire team's sentiments. "They know it's more than just a job; more than just getting a paycheck," Dawn confirms. Indeed, it is a cause, a vision, and a lifestyle that truly unites her team in mission and purpose, allowing for a degree of commitment to their clients' success that is as sincere as it is rare and as powerful as it is poignant.

Deepak Hathiramani

The Sacrifice behind Success

There are some memories that never leave us. Deepak Hathiramani, for instance, will never forget the night in 1967 when his father came into his room and told him to grab what he could. Five years old at the time, he can still recall escaping into the night, evading the civil war upsetting the country by escaping to a French colony in Africa called Cameroon. It was common in that time and place for parents to send their children out of the country for better schooling, and so his parents packed the young boy's bags for India. "I have very distinct memories of what I was wearing the day I left my parents," Deepak remembers. "It was very difficult to leave them." After Deepak's departure, the family later moved to Spain, where he remembers his first time visiting them. "We went to buy eggs at the grocery store and my mother would buy the ones with cracked shells because they were five cents cheaper per dozen," he recalls. From an early age, sacrifice became a permanent fixture in his life.

Thankfully, the family had relatives in India who welcomed Deepak into their home, and he was raised by his aunt and grandmother in Bombay as he made the most of the difficult separation from his parents by working hard at school. "My grandmother taught me that integrity and ethics are absolutely paramount," he explains. He remained in India from 1969 until 1983, when his parents urged him to come work for the small tourist business they had started in the Canary Islands. They had built a good quality of life for themselves from their humble beginnings, and they knew Deepak's life would be well provided for through the business.

Deepak, however, could not deny the voice inside him that called for something more. Computers were just becoming a mainstay in world culture, and he was quickly enraptured by the concepts of technology and engineering. Thus, in choosing to sacrifice a reunion with his family and a relatively secure future in the tourism industry, Deepak embraced the possibility of his dreams, remaining in school in India where he received a Bachelors Degree in Physics and Mathematics with a minor in Operations Research. He then received a diploma in Business Management before coming to the U.S. in 1983 to pursue a degree in Computer Science from Austin, Texas. "I wanted to come to the U.S. because it had so much to offer," he recalls. "It's a place where you can start at the very bottom and make it to the very top with few restrictions. If you work hard, you get rewarded."

Hoping to gain valuable experience that would help him start his own business in the future, he found employment at a startup company called Cinnabar Software shortly after graduation. The five-employee enterprise essentially built software designed to test other software, and Deepak's work often brought him into Washington, D.C., allowing him to gain a nuanced understanding and appreciation of the city and its community.

When Cinnabar was later sold to a publicly traded company after a fruitless attempt to raise external financing, Deepak transitioned into a role at Netrix Corporation in 1989. At that time the company employed thirty people and drew $300 thousand in revenue per year. After Netrix brought in a new CEO, however, it grew quite suddenly and quite exponentially, bringing the company to $30 million in revenue within three years. It quickly became the fastest growing company on the NASDAQ market, boasting a tremendous public offering in October of 1992. They say what goes up must come down, however, and Netrix (now NX Network) was no exception, suddenly plummeting to become the fastest falling company on the NASDAQ market.

"Once that happened, I decided it was now or never," Deepak recalls. His work had focused primarily on the technology aspect of matters while at Cinnabar and Netrix, but this had not prevented him from absorbing valuable leadership insight as each company rose and fell with the tides of success and failure. Though he had initially formed Vistronix in 1990, the initiative didn't pick up momentum until 1992 as it ventured forth into the commercial sector. The early years were not always easy for the fledgling company, and Deepak will never forget the night his wife offered to mortgage her jewelry to help. Once again, sacrifice left a permanent imprint on his memory, reminding him of the true value of love and progress over the material.

Soon after that, however, Deepak spun the helm and began to pursue government space instead—a move that heralded tremendous success for the company and for the people who had sacrificed to keep it afloat. With 325 employees today and an annual revenue pool above $40 million, Vistronix now directs all of its energies toward filling this role as a federal systems integrator.

Vistronix currently serves its clientele through four major spheres. The first is its Geospatial Decision Support, of which the Department of Agriculture and the EPA are two key clients. This is followed by its Information Management branch, which focuses on records management expertise designed to navigate the government's complicated regulatory and compliance requirements. Deepak defines the third area as Independent Verification and Validation, which serves as an objective third party that provides oversight to ensure proper implementation when large systems are being launched. Vistronix's final area of focus, then, is Information Technology Service Management, which assists government agencies in operating its technology infrastructure. To this end, Vistronix is primarily a civilian government focused agency whose primary goal is to leverage technology to aid government agencies in accomplishing their missions.

As Deepak explains, the most pivotal asset to his business along this path to success has been finding the right people for his team. "We're in the people business," he says. "Having the right team members will make you, and having the wrong team members will break you. We learned that lesson the hard way." One team of employees in particular was able to get the company to a certain point but proved unable to take it any further, and as a business owner and entrepreneur, Deepak tended to hope the problem would resolve itself on its own. It didn't, however, and he was forced to take strides to right that particular wrong. Now a strong team builder who places strong emphasis on the fundamental objectives of collaboration and passion supplemented by the integrity and ethics ingrained in him by his family, Deepak's ability to assemble powerful task forces has been honed by both inherent skill and lived experience.

Another turning point along the path toward Vistronix's success was Deepak's realization that a mixture of work and family was not necessarily in the best interest of either party involved. He discovered this after realizing that many of his employees would never view his wife, who worked on the company's finances, as anyone other than "the boss's spouse." Not only would this limit her in her development through its lack of objectivity and openness, but it also thwarted the presence of a clear boundary between work strife and home strife. As a result, Mrs. Hathiramani left Vistronix to pursue her passions in a more neutral environment. Still, Mrs. Hathiramani remains a pivotal force in Deepak's personal and professional development. "I agree with the saying that behind every successful man is a woman," Deepak reflects, "but it is probably more true to say that alongside every successful man is an even better woman. In my case, she may even be a few steps ahead of me," he laughs.

Deepak further identifies a third turning point, which is the company's decision to focus on developing a few targeted core competencies rather than trying to do everything for everybody. "You've got to be known for something," he emphasizes.

Internal expertise, however, can only take a company so far without the assistance and regulation afforded through outside perspectives and guidance, and it is for this reason that Deepak decided to form a Board of Advisors in 2000 to promote Vistronix through periods of transition and growth. Comprised of various senior leaders in the DC metro area who have achieved notable success in their own careers, the board has been instrumental in developing the company's market savvy as well as its strategic relationships. While the board meets quarterly, the ample interaction between members and managers throughout the year continues to supplement the business in each interim.

In addition to the guidance afforded through the Board of Directors, Deepak has taken great strides throughout his professional career to continue his education through various means, including supplemental business management courses at Dartmouth University. He also belongs to a CEO peer group called CEO Project, an offshoot from Inc. 500 that has been tremendously effective in helping him grow along an avenue of both a personal and professional nature.

In advising young entrepreneurs today, Deepak takes an approach that is thoroughly informed by his experiences growing up around the world in communities vastly different from the U.S. landscape. "As a society, we've become very materialistic," Deepak observes. "Money is important, but if you look back on a career, the component that lends a considerable amount of satisfaction is ultimately how you impacted the lives of others. How good was your quality of life? Did you get a chance to work for something you were passionate about and to have an impact on society?"

In many ways, this advice echoes not only his humble roots, but also the struggles he's faced along the way in striving to establish a balance between work and home life. Not having the opportunity to spend enough time with his parents marks a notable regret for him, as does a similar lack of adequate quality time with his three sons in the past. Undoubtedly, achieving an optimal work/life balance can be a lifelong process, particularly when starting a business requires so much time, energy, and sacrifice. Deepak, however, resembles a concerted and resolved effort to overcome this challenge, firmly committed to spinning sacrifice into success in all aspects of his story.

John Hellerman

The Perpetual Forward Thinker

Like a small Chess master always thinking five moves ahead, ten-year-old John Hellerman considered his options. The current exchange rate for converting American dollars to Jamaican dollars was 1.8, meaning the ten dollars his father had given him to spend at the resort would automatically turn into eighteen. However, he had just overheard that a group of men would be outside in the courtyard exchanging two Jamaican dollars for every American dollar, which would leave him with twenty. Of course the boy appeared in the courtyard, taking advantage of this stellar deal and budgeting out for his bounty of t-shirts and beads. But what about jet ski rides? John had already decided against spending his money on such frivolity, aware that his twenty bucks would have only afforded him a couple short-lived minutes of glory. Instead, he sought employment with the jet ski man for the week of his family vacation, hosing off life jackets in exchange for free rides every hour or so. The boy had it made. Or rather, he made it himself.

Now the Partner and Co-Founder of Hellerman Baretz Communications, among the top crisis litigation PR firms in the country, John's style of strategic forward thinking has served him well in the years since that Jamaican business trip of his youth. He had always exhibited the will and capacity to have a clear and discerning idea of his own path and preferences, even at age ten when he was given information about Reagan and Carter during their campaigns for presidency. In fact, John hoped to pursue a career in political campaigning himself until he realized the chances of him achieving the kind of clout and impact he hoped for were too slim to invest his whole life in. "Even in that kind of an atmosphere, money calls the shots," he observes now. "If money is calling the shots, you can either be subservient to that money and hope it works out in the end for you, or you can be the guy with the money." It was with this success as his objective that he sought to expedite his track to success, gathering the PR and marketing skill and experience necessary to launch a business that would aim to represent professionals with a specialization in the legal field.

John then met Spencer Baretz in August of 2002 while doing some work for clients in New York City. He had gone into business on his own in September of the previous year, and the two seemed to share the same vision and focus. Spencer was a former practicing attorney and had been doing a lot of writing for some firms in the city, while John had been working with attorneys for more than twelve years and had a wealth of marketing and PR experience as well. The two entrepreneurs assembled a business plan over the course of the fall that they then implemented in early February of 2003, thus initiating Hellerman Baretz from the realm of ideas into the realm of reality.

Since that day, Hellerman Baretz has excelled in providing competitive and compelling promotional resources and assistance to professional service firms. They perform a host of duties for their partners—primarily lawyers—to promote their expertise within a given niche, be it healthcare, insurance, new government regulations, etcetera. Thirty percent of their business comes through referrals for litigation consulting from lawyers; hence, their work tends to cluster around litigation PR and crisis management.

Hellerman Baretz is truly a product of changing times, as the litigation scene has come a long way from the days of tight-lipped silence in which clients were advised not to talk to the press. In the last decade or two, the industry now knows that companies must maintain their reputation regardless of what happens in the court room. "The realization was that, in these exceptionally charged and public situations, the interest of the company, its shareholders, and its employees has to be represented and advocated for—not only in the court, but in the court of public opinion as well," John explains.

John's experience in the industry draws from an extensive history that first commenced soon after he began college at Tulane University, where he worked on several political campaigns and then served as the Director of Marketing for a small timeshare hotel in the French Quarter of New Orleans. Eager to develop relationships with his professors, he also founded a talk show airing on a local cable and closed circuit channel called *Point of View* in which he would invite his future professors to appear as guests to discuss a political topic of the day. "I liked being able to ask the questions and offer my own insight," John explains, "and it was a great way to get to know my professors before having class with them and to set myself apart in some way."

Though he had been working toward a political science major, it was shortly through his time at Tulane that John first thought he wanted to be a political consultant, running and marketing campaigns. He had acquired a strong political science background from his classes and had read a lot about Columbia College in Chicago, which was known for its media and communications expertise. What's more, the school's instructors were primarily business owners and professionals who were actually out in the community practicing the subject matter of their courses. "I was very conscious of the fact that transferring was a big risk, but I felt like Columbia was a place where I could meet people who could later hire me," John explains. "I knew I needed to make it work." He did, in fact, make it work, graduating and winning a position as the primary writer for a political campaign. Although John's candidate eventually lost, John wrote many ads and fundraising letters and was noticed by a lawyer, who extended an job offer for somewhat of a legal writing position. John tried his hand at that for a while before accepted employment at a small PR firm in Chicago that serviced a wide variety of clients, from restaurant chefs to hospitality entities to lawyers.

This experience served as an excellent entry point into Jaffe Associates, the PR firm based in Washington, DC that had done the first real display advertisement for a defense firm. "I've still never seen a better campaign than that one," John reminisces of the spread that first earned Jaffe a name for itself in the legal world. John chose to transition over to Jaffe because he had enjoyed working with lawyers previously, and doing so enabled him to witness the incredible ballooning that transformed the industry soon thereafter. "It had only been legal to market for lawyers since the late 70's, and nobody actually did it until the mid 80's. I got into it around 1993, and I feel lucky that I got to watch the industry develop," he reports.

John eventually left Jaffe along with one other employee and helped him found a crisis communications litigation firm called Levick Strategic Communications. "I was a cocky kid who thought I was leaving Jaffe to be a founder," he laughs. "The problem was, I was a founder and not an owner." Being so close yet somehow far away from implementing his vision actually helped to cement that vision in John's mind. "I would think to myself what I would and wouldn't do the same if I was in charge," he recalls, creating a firmer framework for Hellerman Baretz Communications once it came into existence several years later.

The company currently draws the majority of its clients from the American Lawyer-200, a list of the two hundred largest law firms in the country. Of that list, John has worked for about eighty firms, or 60% of the top 100, earning him a solid reputation amongst the community. The company currently has ten employees and has been on the Inc 5000 list for three consecutive years now. They've also maintained a growth rate of 28 percent over the past decade, with employee growth trailing that at ten percent. John's task force thus consists of several senior people and a team of primarily younger employees, whom he enjoys mentoring and who pick up their skills exceptionally quickly through the company's strong protocols and service checklists.

But what exactly makes John's vision so unique and Hellerman Baretz Communications, in turn, so successful? The singularity of his design draws in large part from the surprisingly fresh and sincere perspective on his industry he's cultivated over the years. "Networking never appealed to me," says John. "I don't want to represent people based on who they know. For me, marketing is more substantive—it's about relationship building. I help my client enrich a relationship by generating content they can share when they're talking to someone so they don't come up empty handed." Furthermore, for Hellerman Baretz Commnications, it's about advocacy. "We help our clients influence a discussion, promoting ideas and solutions instead of just their expertise." Finally, John believes in the importance of lending a creative element to his products despite a certain lack of emphasis on creativity in the legal field. Though this personal touch may go unnoticed by his clients, it is likely that the clients of his clients don't miss it.

The consistent theme permeating John's story, then, is strategy. Much of his success stems from maintaining a strategic mindset as a default way of thinking rather than a tool utilized only in obvious situations. Consider, for example, his utilization of a team retreat he participated in just after being hired at Jaffe. Essentially his first experience in a real corporate environment, John identified five of his 20 colleagues to be real movers and shakers. "I then made myself a mental note that if one of those five ever came looking for something from me, I would drop everything and make sure it got done," John explains. "They had influence. They had an air about them. And it's this kind of person you want giving high recommendations about you."

Consequently, John's primary piece of advice to a young entrepreneur entering the business world today revolves around the importance of setting one's self apart. "Don't be average," he instructs. "It doesn't take much to be above average. There's a difference between book smart and business smart, so figure out which one will take you farther and focus on that." John himself looks more for individuals who exhibit real world, applicable reasoning skills coupled with curiosity, brightness, and a willingness to trust, absorb, and grow. "Once you've got the job," says John, "make yourself invaluable—just dazzle. When you're invaluable, you call the shots." And of course, each of these tenets is only leant more value through the ability to operate with the end goal in mind, allowing one to proactively adjust their gait to the bold yet rational strides it takes to get there.

Adonis Hoffman

Global Transformation through Corporate Citizenship

His mother was a seamstress and his father was a construction worker, neither of whom made it past high school. Still, education was of paramount importance in the Hoffman family, and Adonis always knew he would go to college. From his father he drew a strong sense of grounding, and from his mother he drew the power of dreaming. And later, after seeing the world and the mechanics of its functioning, he would cement a sense of responsibility that extends far beyond the individual, and farther still beyond the impact of government. Now the Managing Director of Leadership Counsel, a unique and innovative firm poised at the cutting edge of corporate responsibility and reputation consultancy, Adonis Hoffman uses each and every experience in his vast arsenal of memory to address the escalating importance of corporations to act as positive and accountable entities in the today's global landscape.

As Adonis describes, an astounding 35 of the world's top economies are corporations, ranking higher than many countries and governments and thus suggesting that business now wields a certain power in society that was once reserved for governments and nation-states. With this tremendous power, however, comes tremendous responsibility. To date, Adonis's work has been a nuanced and comprehensive approach to guiding this reality in a positive, compelling, and unprecedented direction, with Leadership Counsel aiding clients in defining comprehensive corporate responsibility solutions.

At its essence, corporate responsibility is the way companies adhere to certain principles, policies, and practices that affect the way they do business. With an implicit link to local or even global communities, it pertains to the manner in which a company contributes time, resources, and talent—in short, how a company conducts itself as a citizen within society. Encapsulating areas such as philanthropy, accountability, citizenship, diversity, and ethics, it is ultimately the act of doing business with a respect and appreciation for the industry and community in which it thrives, acting in the best interest of "the whole" even if such integrity warrants a larger price tag for the company itself.

And yet, while the immediate cost of being a responsible corporate citizen may appear larger at face value, current research indicates that the choice to commit to such ethical standards is a marketing tool that has gained momentum as consumers adopt a larger sense of responsibility of their own. Studies indicate that more consumers are looking for corporations to be responsible citizens in our society, actively giving back to both the local and global community. "All things being equal," Adonis explains, "companies are often distinguished from competition based on the nature of their commitment to corporate responsibility." Research even indicates that some consumers are willing to pay more for a product that guarantees such values.

The other primary crux of Leadership Counsel's service model is its focus on corporate reputation. Of course, it seems only logical that every company should be concerned about the image it portrays to the outside world in terms of the quality and value it boasts, the way it treats employees, and the ways in which it gives back to the community. However, actually advocating these principles is easier said than done. In this sense, corporate reputation is inextricably linked with corporate responsibility. Leadership Counsel, then, aims to assist organizations of all sizes to understand, implement, and then market these issues in a more efficient and effective way.

"For companies that are on a sound trajectory and even those that are not, we believe we can bring some leadership and counsel to their management team, executives, and boards," Adonis explains. "I truly believe that businesses in American society are fundamentally a good thing, creating opportunity, wealth, and prosperity. However, businesses also get a bad reputation when they neglect to do the right thing. The goal of Leadership Counsel, then, is to bring a multifaceted frame of reference to the issues at hand that will help a company do its work better through accomplishing its objective of being a better corporate entity and of getting proper credit from appropriate third parties." In essence, the consultancy serves to help leaders chart the course from their current latitude and longitude to where they hope to be, lending value to society and benefitting communities along the way.

Adonis first launched Leadership Counsel as a two-person consulting firm in 1997, collaborating with his partner, Victor Frazer, a longstanding friend, lawyer, and former member of the U.S. Congress with extensive experience in interior corporate dynamics. "Because we're so small, it's very important to us that the service we provide is strategy and not implementation," Adonis stresses. "Unlike a PR firm, we don't write press releases, develop media, or address campaigning. Rather, our unique selling proposition is our commitment to providing the overall strategy." This is done through meetings with a company's C-level executives to present key decision makers with strategic outlines and observations—sometimes highly-sensitive—about their business and market.

A typical strategy might set out guidelines and advice for developing important relationships with environmental groups, activists, academics, think tanks, civil rights organizations, community leaders , and policymakers, for example. It might then be followed with instructions and suggestions for communicating messages to important influentials in government, media and industry. Adonis could not hope to provide the lenses necessary to accomplish such a sweeping task, however, without an extraordinary background and wealth of industry experience to inform his perspective—a journey that began in childhood but was continued after his graduation from Princeton University.

The year was 1976, and he had completed a management training program at Bank of America in California and accepted a full-time position there. He worked at the bank for a year before seizing an opportunity to explore his interest in local and state politics that had originally been ignited by a high school internship with Los Angeles Mayor Tom Bradley. With that, he joined the staff of the Lieutenant Governor of California, Mervyn Dymally, the state's first African American to hold that office. This experience exposed Adonis to people whose involvement in community issues and interests lent a lasting sense of public service to his repertoire of interests, explaining much of his commitment today. He then remained in state government for four years until Governor Dymally ran successfully for Congress in 1980.

With this victory, Adonis accepted the invitation to move to Washington and work for the new Congressman on Capitol Hill as his Legislative Director, attending night classes at Georgetown University Law Center at the same time. Coming to the nation's capital opened the young man's eyes to both national and international issues, and in 1984, he left the Hill to work for Gray and Company, a predominantly Republican lobbying and public communications firm representing foreign governments and large companies. As one of the firm's few Democrats, he recalls that much of his work was involved in helping these clients present a better public image and improve their reputations on

Capitol Hill. "I sometimes felt as though we glossed over things, , and I wanted to provide something deeper, more tangible, more solid," Adonis explains.

After finishing law school in 1986, he practiced law at a national law firm as a legislative, regulatory and corporate lawyer, until he again answered the call of government service in 1990. The Congressman he originally worked for had become Chairman of a key subcommittee on the House Committee on Foreign Affairs and wanted Adonis to serve as the staff director, which he eagerly accepted. In this capacity, he had the extraordinary opportunity to travel extensively throughout Asia, Africa, and the Middle East. Though his journeys were fraught with wonder, he also found the repeated exposure to abject poverty to be life-changing. "You can't see something like that and walk away unaffected," he explains. "I wanted to make a change through my career somehow, but I didn't know exactly what to do yet."

When the Congressman retired in 1993, Adonis returned to law practice but couldn't shake the urge to do policy work, so he found his way into the Carnegie Endowment for International Peace, a leading foreign policy think tank in Washington, where he focused on democracy, governance and international law, especially in Africa and developing countries. It was only after leaving Carnegie that he felt he had acquired the plethora of experience necessary to launch a successful firm, and with that, Leadership Counsel was born.

It is interesting to note that, in its fledgling stages, Leadership Counsel also focused on foreign government development, assisting countries as they attempted to develop effective communications with Washington and as they worked through massive societal shifts. In several instances, for example, Adonis assembled teams to go to newly-democratic countries to observe their elections, providing guidance and reports for how to improve their constitutions and commercial code.

In 1997, as a result of his international work, Adonis received an invitation from the Chairman of the FCC, Bill Kennard, to work on the chairman's new international initiative to bring transparency and accountability to developing countries in the areas of communications. "I really appreciated this opportunity because it launched me into international communications work, and from there I was able to move into communications policy and merger work involving cable and internet companies regulated through the FCC," he recalls. He left the FCC in 2000 to serve as Senior Vice President and legal counsel for the American Association of Advertising Agencies for eleven years, whence he returned to Leadership Counsel with—quite literally—a world's worth of new knowledge and skill. He then began marketing the company as a strategic management consultancy with its current niche focus, shifting away from the broader interests it had pursued previously.

Despite all his travel and experience, however, Adonis insists that the attitude of altruism and stewardship so prevalent in his mission was instilled long ago by the institutions and experiences most familiar to America's youth: his high school, his church, and a sweeping generational mentality. "I came of age in the 1970s during a time fertile with debate about the role of government and business in society," he recalls. "You can't divorce the spirit of the times from your own experience, and I always felt that I had to do something with some redeeming social value with my life. It wasn't until I got older that I figured out how to combine my need to contribute to society with my need for a sustaining profession that would provide both the social impact and financial independence I hoped for."

In advising young entrepreneurs entering the workforce today, then, Adonis recommends a considerable devotion of time to analyzing one's personal values and their roots. A reflective exercise of this nature will assist in solidifying one's character and will thus be instrumental in the subsequent use of these values to identify a career that will allow them to be expressed professionally. "After all, beauty is only skin deep, but character goes all the way to the bone," Adonis quotes.

And isn't that what it's all about, after all? Not a sense of detached responsibility, not a mere façade kept in the interest of attracting the growing socially-minded consumer population for personal gain, but an ideology sunk into the very framework of a corporate entity? Adonis's latest book, entitled *Doing Good: The New Rules of Corporate Responsibility, Conscience, and Character*, was published in the fall of 2010, but his vision of making this ideal a mainstream mainstay doesn't stop there. Indeed, the publication is only the most recent installment as the impact of a legacy begins to flesh out: one in which the commercial players shaping our societies today are challenged to move beyond basic corporate responsibility and toward an evolution of true conscience and character.

BERNHARDT

WEALTH MANAGEMENT

David Iannarone

The Scope of Reflection

"Dave, you know when to zig and when to zag," proclaimed the baseball coach in admiration.

A high schooler at the time, David Iannarone didn't exactly know what the man meant. Now the President of CWCapital Asset Management, he has since come to understand that zigging and zagging pertain to a kind of intuitive reflexivity lent by perceptive self-observation and reflection. It means swift and well-executed reaction based on the careful, calculated, thoughtful pre-consideration that allows one to learn a subject inside and out. The youngest of three siblings, he grew up a listener and observer, honing his ability to pick up on subtle facts and cues. Over the years, Dave has approached the path of his life in much the same way he had once approached the path of a baseball, using his reflections and objectives to determine when to zig and when to zag.

This is not to say that he always knew what he wanted to do in life. Rather, he developed a general idea of the realm he wanted to head towards and trusted his innate reflexivity to keep him aimed in the right direction. Thus, although he wasn't certain whether he ultimately wanted to be a lawyer, Dave decided to pursue a law degree after graduating from college. When he attained his JD from Villanova and noted that he was more interested in transactional law as opposed to litigation, he took a position with the finance group at Kaye Scholer, LLP, a premier law firm in New York City. True to his natural form, he constantly reviewed and reflected upon his current position in the context of future goals. "In the back of my mind, I was always trying to build my resume towards more of a business focus," he recalls. After three years at Kaye Scholer, he had learned the ins and outs of running a transaction from beginning to end.

With the running theme of business orientation in the back of his mind, he then took a position with Citibank. Enjoying a constant stream of new learning experiences and analytical demands, Dave remembers the first six months of his employment as a thrilling time. The influx of opportunity, however, was promptly cut off with the thrift crisis and real estate debacle that came with the 1980s' denouement. "I was always told it was a cradle-to-grave type of job, and frankly the grave part scared me," Dave laughs now.

With Citibank entering a period of relative isolationism, he was afforded new perspective on his position. "It was what I *thought* I was looking for—pretty controlled, pretty orderly. But in the end it was pretty boring as well," he concedes. Identifying the personal need for a challenge, he made a zig and focused his energies on earning his advanced law degree at New York University. With the heightened business focus of the LLM, he had the opportunity to learn about disclosures, verbiage, shareholder voting procedure, director appointment procedure, and the rules of directorship. With its fundamental focus in business law, the program figured ideally into his grand plan.

Growing restless of New York City, however, Dave felt it was time to zag and found himself answering an advertisement in the Wall Street Journal for a position with the Resolution Trust Corporations (RTC) in Washington, DC. After transferring his LLM program from NYU to Georgetown and hopping a train south, he suddenly found himself leading a brand new life teeming with fascinating people and work. Heading up the national program for residential securitization, he introduced the policies and procedures for assembling loans from banks and selling them to Fannie Mae and Freddie Mac. Noting that tax law drives so much of the business landscape, he ultimately earned his LLM with a focus in Securities and Tax.

Ever introspective and self-aware, however, Dave eventually came to feel that his duties at the RTC were no longer stretching his capacities. It was around this time that a headhunter happened to mention a job opening at CRIIMI MAE Inc. that entailed a smorgasbord of varying duties, promising extensive experience in public and commercial real estate finance company happenings. The job was perfect for Dave, and he worked there quite contentedly until the company filed for bankruptcy. Despite entertaining notions of starting his own entrepreneurial venture, he eventually succumbed to the advice that seeing CRIIMI through the bankruptcy process would afford him a tremendous learning experience; thus, he stayed on and served as chief restructuring officer.

Once CRIIMI had successfully navigated through bankruptcy and Dave had fulfilled his subsequent two-year contract of employment, he departed to assume the role of Director of Capital Markets with Allied Capital Corporation in 2003. The opportunity diverged somewhat from the commercial real estate finance sector he was used to, and he enjoyed the challenge of applying his seasoned expertise to a new sector. "You get smarter as you get older, and the one thing you learn to do is trust your instincts a little more," he explains now. He declined other job offers to remain with Allied until switching over to the CWCapital Asset Management (CWCAM) platform in July of 2005.

CWCAM manages distressed assets, a far more complex and fascinating process than first meets the eye. The field has evolved and merged over the past twenty years to demand dual expertise in both commercial real estate and finance—true Renaissance individuals capable of understanding the subtle yet comprehensive nuance and analytics behind property valuation and loan processes. This is further compounded by the necessary consideration of the investors behind the loans, the broader real estate lending market trends at work, and the legal component underpinning the enterprise.

"The most fascinating part about it is you're not sitting in your office or cubicle working through these ideas, numbers, and conclusions," Dave explains. "You've got to interface with people, negotiating and fighting for the best deal for the lender." This implies the importance not only of impeccable industry knowledge, but of iron negotiation skills as well.

In his first three years with CWCAM, Dave and his team's primary goal was establishing a premier commercial mortgage loan shop. With his hallmark trait of reflection, Dave sensed that the spoilage of commercial loans was imminent, so his efforts took on a proactive and preparatory vision. Training, systems, and processes became key considerations for the business, as well as the art of swift and efficient decision-making. Each asset manager was equipped with optimal levels of support, with junior employees aiding senior associates and gaining the knowledge to become associate asset managers themselves in the future. "When commercial loans went bad, people were surprised by our preparedness," Dave remembers. "This was not by accident, but by design." Because of his vision and foresight, CWCAM was prepared to staff up and scale to manage more assets, growing from 65 employees in 2008 to over 140 employees now, securing their renown as a premier special servicing platform.

Beyond this foresight, CWCAM is rendered so unique amidst this developing and fast-paced atmosphere by its capacity to offer high-powered staff with deep industry experience. "We're diverse," says Dave.

"We have the real estate guys and the workout guys, and we have very strong technology. Within this, our true value lies in our attitude and how we work together to develop a level of knowledge that is unparalleled."

In reviewing his journey to this point, perhaps the most pronounced and compelling aspect of Dave's story has been the compounding nature of self-knowledge. Unsure of the exact path for him, he was able to find it through observing his skills and passions and then working toward them until a clear goal solidified. The journey in turn granted him further self-knowledge, as he was able to monitor his own responses to new situations and obstacles. While working at Allied, for example, he was asked whether his skills were more transactional or operational oriented. Though at the time he believed he was more transactional, he has since reclassified himself an operations guy. "I like creating a goal and helping everyone grow in the same direction to get to that goal," he explains. Allowing this kind of organic growth of the self instead of trying to force one's skills into a predetermined mold guarantees a much more natural and steadfast success. "Really, you need to learn who you are and then pick things that you're good at," he emphasizes.

Thus, one cannot expect to land in the perfect professional situation immediately upon entering the workforce. While navigating along the path to your ultimate goal, Dave reiterates the importance of continuous evaluation of situation and self in order to stay on track. "When participating in your first jobs, ask yourself if you're learning," he encourages. "Then, look at those jobs and ask what parts you liked." He also emphasizes the importance of learning as many skills as you can, even those that seem repetitive, boring, or obtuse. "People often feel that they want to take on more responsibility in a new job, but your boss doesn't want to give you the hard tasks if you aren't demonstrating that you can do the easy tasks," Dave reminds us.

Just as he is continually drawing on a plethora of sources to inform his reflections, Dave's journey of personal and professional evolution is far from over. "I see the future as bigger and better," he says, referring to CWCAM's prospects. In his own development and in his advice to others, he remains acutely aware of the continuous opportunity to excel and strives to never drop the ball. "People don't seem to realize that we're always getting graded," he remarks. "Develop the network around you just as much as the network above you, because your co-workers will all move elsewhere in the professional world and will maintain lasting impressions of you." Dave holds that such impressions are derived from one's quality of work, quantity of work, and the attitude employed while doing that work, so he monitors these facets constantly to ensure lasting success. It's all part of the art of zigging and zagging: discovering yourself and carving out your own road toward professional achievement and personal fulfillment.

Shiv Krishnan

The Cyclical Nature of Success

Though he's now a successful entrepreneur living the American Dream, Shiv Krishnan will never forget the man dressed all in white who arrived one day at the door of his modest house in Madras, India. At twelve years of age, Shiv was surprised to see the 6'2" tall man suddenly fall to his knees at his grandfather's feet in a gesture of respect. Shiv's grandfather had dedicated sixty years of his life to the education of over five thousand of the city's impoverished children, and this man had been one of those kids. He had just gotten a call from the Prime Minister of India appointing him Chief Justice of the Supreme Court, and the man immediately hopped in his car to come pay homage to the elder who had changed his life.

"*That* is the power of education," Shiv proclaims today. Now the Founder and CEO of INDUS Corporation, an information technology (IT) solutions firm servicing the Federal government, the topic remains paramount to his life philosophy and philanthropic pursuits. "In education, you don't impart money; you impart opportunity," he explains. As someone born and raised in a part of the world where both resources and opportunity were oftentimes so scant, Shiv could discern from an early age the true magnitude of the idea and has since held it as paramount in his mind.

Shiv's father was the finance director for a large engineering and power generation equipment company, a job which required constant relocation to remote areas of India with little infrastructure and few educational opportunities. When Shiv reached the age of five, his parents decided to send him to live with his grandparents in Madras, where he would have access to education and stability. Life remained relatively calm for him until he attended college and had the opportunity to meet a new cast of people that would begin molding him into the man he is today.

It wasn't long before Shiv befriended a fellow student whose grandfather had been a poor boy peddling newspapers but grew up to build the largest newspaper chain in India—an empire that spanned the entire country. "I was taken with the work ethic; with the singular focus; with the energy involved in building an enterprise and creating that sheer volume of jobs and opportunity," he marvels. His entrepreneurial flame had been sparked, and to feed it, he organized an entrepreneurship seminar at his college, bringing in speakers from small businesses to teach about the process of founding a company and the governmental support available for such an endeavor.

After receiving his Bachelors degree in Chemical Engineering, he immediately relocated to the U.S. to commence graduate school at Clarkson University in upstate New York in 1979. "My initial thinking was to return to India after a couple of years, but it's all about exposure," says Shiv. Taken with American society's unparalleled attitude of openness to new ideas and entrepreneurship, he accepted a job at the Commonwealth of Virginia upon receiving his degree. It was here that he first practiced the idea of using computers to write programs that might increase productivity. After noting initial work by the Environmental Protection Agency (EPA) to develop computerized models to predict dispersion of chemicals polluting the atmosphere, he started utilizing his own coursework and Chemical Engineering background to do the same. He supplemented his efforts with computer courses and started using computers to solve problems at a time when few others had begun to do such a thing.

Shiv then left the Commonwealth to assume a position with Versar, Inc., an environmental consulting company servicing organizations like the EPA and American Management Systems (AMS), a premier IT and systems company at the time. He later transitioned over to AMS and assumed employment there in 1984, the same year he married his beloved wife, Meena. Then, in 1987, Shiv received a particularly interesting offer from an acquaintance who owned a research and development company with about a hundred employees consulting to NASA. The man wanted to expand into the Washington metro area and thought Shiv was perfect for the job. Leaping to the challenge, Shiv launched the Washington branch from the spare bedroom of his apartment. Three years later, he had grown the branch to a hundred people and was doing $5 million in revenue, later establishing offices in Boston and North Carolina as well. The company, however, did not like the stress and inconsistency associated with consulting projects and decided to focus on NASA R&D—a confinement that didn't jive with Shiv's intuition and entrepreneurial inclinations.

As technology continued to evolve and present new tools for him to leverage in providing solutions to various companies, Shiv began to consider starting a business of his own. Meena had a solid job at Bell Atlantic, which would later become Verizon, and the two reflected on how they were truly living the American Dream: a nice house in the suburbs, two cars, and a beautiful daughter with another on the way. Recognizing that the risk would be harder and harder to take the more they succumbed to a daily grind, and with Meena's support and encouragement, he took the plunge in 1993, and INDUS Corporation was born. Three years later, he bought the business he had been working in previously, bringing INDUS's size to about sixty employees. After participating in a number of commercial contracts, Shiv then decided to target government contracts instead, leveraging earlier relationships to make the transition. INDUS has since evolved exponentially, now bringing in $100 million in revenue annually.

Much of the company's success stems from that pivotal decision to switch the focus of its clientele, and it's no mystery why. The U.S. government is perhaps the largest conceivable customer there is, spending approximately $525 billion per year on a vast array of products and services. Close to $100 billion of this is spent on IT alone. This figure is steadily increasing as the tremendously competitive economic climate tends toward more efficient and intelligent methods of work. Technology, in turn, stands out as the best and most cost-effective option in terms of improving productivity and solving problems. Thus, the U.S. government's focus on technology has helped to keep it at the forefront of leadership and innovation.

Shiv remarks, however, that beyond its sheer breadth and the complex rules and regulations involved in the bidding process, the government is no different from any other client. "The conversation is simple," Shiv says. "What are your business challenges?" He then analyzes these challenges and considers the possible technology and solutions, whether available or conceivable, that might increase productivity or cut costs, allowing them to better serve the citizens of the U.S.

But what allows INDUS to distinguish itself and carve a piece of success from this industry? The company is rendered so unique, first of all, through its specialization in particular technology areas. Because IT is so broad, they focus on the areas in which they excel—namely, geospatial and data management. "We are very good at managing the enormous amounts of data coming in and then converting it to meaningful information that can be further distilled into actionable intelligence for our customers," Shiv explains. INDUS further stands out from its competition to the degree that it assists in managing the software assets of their customers when they lack the skill sets required to do so themselves. These services are further enhanced through its ability to advise and implement security solutions, safeguarding their clients' infrastructures against the escalating threats and vulnerabilities plaguing the cyber landscape today.

Beyond expertise, INDUS is known for its excellence in customer service, which is critical in the government contracting world where past performance plays such a vital role in establishing credibility and winning future bids. Their reputation is further confirmed by their achievement of the latest international certifications for quality processes and standards and overall industry best practices, and they maintain the credentials that are very specific to their particular areas of expertise within their industry. "These certifications let the government know that our service is of the highest quality and that they can put a lot of faith in our company," Shiv explains. "But still, at the end of the day, our quality is based on our ability to attract and retain the best people," he concedes. INDUS currently employs a workforce of approximately 450.

"My biggest success has not been building a $100 million company," says Shiv. "Rather, it is being able to impact so many peoples' lives in a very positive way and being able to have an impact on the overall community as a good corporate citizen." Keenly cognizant of the symbiotic relationship existing between company and community, he stresses the give-and-take of the dynamic. "It is important for a company like INDUS to give back to the community in terms of time and funding so that the community can continue to enhance itself," he explains. "A vibrant community will attract talented and fulfilled individuals, who will in turn provide a good hiring pool for companies like INDUS. High-quality companies are thus attracted to the community and compelled to invest in it, perpetuating the cycle."

In advising young entrepreneurs today, Shiv's primary tenet is to follow your passion. He follows up on this with an urging to identify one's strengths and to continue to practice and hone these talents. "If you can create that kind of focus in your life," he says, "you can achieve tremendous things." The relevance of this advice cannot be underscored enough in this age of unparalleled noise and distraction, all of which threaten to clutter one's focus with extraneous considerations.

In achieving this level of excellence, however, one must also seek to understand the paramount importance of risk. "You gain a lot by giving up a lot," he explains. "People think that if they give up something, they lose control, but it's to the contrary." Nowhere is this truth more evident than in Shiv's own experience, most notably when he and Meena signed the paperwork for a $250,000 credit line for INDUS. He can still recall the look on Meena's face, as she can recall the look on his, after they left the meeting in which they signed over their home and everything they had worked for throughout the past seventeen years, thinking, "What have we done?" Were it not for their strength of mind to assume these types of risk, INDUS would not be the company it is today.

Through Shiv's advice, the cyclical relationship expressed between company and community is in many ways replicated across generations—an almost poetic truth demonstrated in many ways by his own daughters. After a family trip to India, the two young ladies were struck by the very same poverty that Shiv's grandfather had dedicated his life to overcoming so many years ago. In characteristic Krishnan fashion, Preeti and Priya have since launched their own foundation, called "Save a Child Now." As executive directors of the enterprise, their impact has already begun to form. Through Shiv's example, then, we are compelled to re-conceptualize of the measure of success, casting it not in dollar signs but in compassion, in community, and in the creation of a better future not only for ourselves and our children, but *through* ourselves and our children.

John Langan

Learning and Leading by Example

Astonished, the woman stared at him for a moment. "You actually read this stuff?" she queried.

John Langan nodded the affirmative. Working an entry-level job at the prominent accounting firm Arthur Andersen, John was not particularly challenged in his position. "I put on a suit and make copies," he had told his family when they inquired about the experience. He soon discovered, however, that though the job entailed largely menial tasks, he could learn much from reading the papers that passed through his hands, trying to understand the more detailed inner-workings of the enterprise. Now, after approaching the senior in charge to ask about the documents, the surprise at his initiative shone on her face. Of course, after the initial shock wore off, she was happy to detail the context for him.

Not only did John seize the opportunity as a chance to learn more about the business, but he also often observed his colleagues and managers to learn more about successful habits and practices. "I would watch how they managed their time and interfaced with the clients," he remembers. "I would watch people who were good at what they did as they moved up the rungs, and I would watch those who were bad at what they did so I could learn what not to do." Now the Principal in Charge of the Washington, DC office of LarsonAllen LLP and of the company's Nonprofit and Government Services Group as well, he still recalls the lessons he learned through this careful observation and weaves such considerations into his own leadership style as he in turn strives to lead by example.

LarsonAllen is a public accounting firm established and headquartered in Minneapolis but currently boasting a strong national presence with offices in twelve states. It draws approximately $230 million in revenue a year, which can be subdivided into the various industries of healthcare, nonprofit and government, manufacturing, construction, financial institutions, and auto dealers. With eighty-five percent of their business concentrated in compliance expected service, they hope to strengthen their consultative opportunities in the future. The current state of the economy has also helped to shape their focus, challenging them to streamline efficiency through their Enterprise Excellence Initiative. Based on the Toyota Lean Model, the initiative focuses on eliminating waste and increasing value through process through modifications on how accounting services, tax returns, and audits are delivered.

Prior to his arrival at LarsonAllen in 2006, John had worked at Arthur Andersen as an auditor for three and a half years. Working in the commercial group at the company's DC office afforded him an eclectic collection of clients that included accounts with Mars, Inc. and Marriot International, Inc. With experiencing spanning the spectrum from a large private company to the transparency and openness of a large public company, augmented with several nonprofit, governmental, and government contracting jobs, he considers his time there as an incredible education for someone just emerging from school. It was also here that he first met Cindy Parks, another auditor who caught his eye and captured his heart.

The company did not permit spouses to work at the same location, so upon his engagement to Cindy, John resigned his post and set about determining his next step. "I felt I could start my own initiative and do well and be more fulfilled," John explains. He entertained a brief stint as a controller but knew after four short months that the highly technical nature of the position did not suit him. Self-identifying with the creative and human aspects of his industry over its quantitative nature, he readily admits that the technical side of the business has never been his passion.

"My passion is in the relationships," he explains. "It's in building a business and bringing skills like communication and time management to the table." His future success stemmed in large part from this intuitive and honest understanding of his strengths and weaknesses, which allows him to embrace his fortes instead of attempting to force himself into a shape that just doesn't fit. His flair and verve instead shine through his people skills, allowing him to forge strong connections and engender trust in others. "Public accounting is the language of business, and we are the translators for our clients," he explains.

With this understanding in mind, he launched Langan Associates, PC, in 1988, which would develop a skilled specialization in nonprofit outsourcing long before the term "outsourcing" was even used. Observing how the nonprofit world was growing ever more complex and required competence in closing books, reporting, and auditing, he found his niche readily identifiable. "The disconnect between the level of competency in the financial management systems of nonprofits and the audit firms that came in to review the work was undeniable," he recalls. "Outsourcing was a natural fit and solution." Langan Associates thus built on its base competency in outsourcing by adding an audit and tax department in 1994, as the demand for those services had increased for local and regional firms when the Big 4 walked away from all but the largest national nonprofits. Overall, this platform was used to grow a $7 million revenue base over an eighteen-year period that included audit, tax and outsourcing service lines.

Despite its ranking in the top thirty of local DC outsourcing firms, the road was not always easy for Langan Associates. Competing for talent against firms that were three times their size presented considerable obstacles that were compounded by their nonprofit niche. "Working in a specific vertical like nonprofits does not make sense for everyone," John concedes, "though it is a very fulfilling client base. So the ability to attract, retain, and develop talent was always our number one issue."

This challenge was countered by the company's introspective edge, which left them ever open to new and innovative opportunities to expand their processes. After doing an internal strategic plan to crystallize the firm's next ten years, it became clear that, in terms of the opportunities enmeshed in their market niche, they were only scratching the surface. In an attempt to mine their prospects, they put together a firm profile in 2005 and met with other firms in the area to develop strategic alliances. LarsonAllen, which was little known on the East coast at the time, was one such firm, boasting strong potential because of its parallel specialization in the nonprofit industry. John appreciated that the firm's employees felt that they had influence over the destiny and direction of the enterprise, lending them a sense of empowerment and commitment. Langan Associates operated with the mindset that outsourcing was a year-round business, demonstrating to LarsonAllen that that they couldn't serve outsourcing with the same talent base reserved for audits.

While most entrepreneurs would say that pursuing their own business posed a considerable risk, John felt otherwise. With his CPA license, he was simply an individual out offering a professional service. However, he knew early on that he wanted to build a legitimate and scalable business rather than pursue a solo and boutique-style practice. "The risk, then, comes over the years as you grow and take on employees, office space, and management," he explains. One risk was in turn followed by another, in which John transitioned over to LarsonAllen.

Fortunately, this risk was met with the most desirable of outcomes—reward. While other industries have suffered with the recent economic downturn, LarsonAllen was among the few national firms with any internal non-acquisition growth. "When times get tight, people can't afford to maintain a status quo in which they aren't getting timely and accurate information with which to make good decisions. The margins are too skinny; they can't accept anything less than knowing exactly where they stand and where they're going from a financial standpoint," he describes.

John credits Susan Stevens, the former Principal in Charge, for her vision, which cultivated LarsonAllen's Nonprofit & Government Group into the firm's second largest industry group and effectively drove home how important and profitable the practice could be. While determining her replacement, she looked to John for both his inherent skill and his prior experience building a business of his own. Known throughout the company as a consensus builder among its leadership, John communicated the vision of the organization effectively and worked well with others.

John's ability to connect people perhaps stem from his childhood, when he grow up as the youngest of four brothers and a sister. He was somewhat of a late bloomer, with his progress and focus stunted by low self-esteem. His brother, Rick, became a tax lawyer and was always very supportive of him, encouraging him to apply himself and achieve his potential before it was too late. After high school, he attended college at the College of Boca Raton—Now Lynn University, where Mr. Langan serves on the Board of Trustees—for two years and decided to take Rick's advice. After making the Dean's List upon graduating with nineteen A's and a C, he describes himself as a big fish in a small pond, finally willing to apply himself and do his part in achieving success. This newfound motivation landed him a scholarship to attend Florida

Atlantic University, where he was drawn to accounting for its promise of flexible and professional prospects upon graduation. Though math was not his passion, Rick explained to him that he had the human skills necessary for the career and could still learn the language and use a calculator. "I liked the idea that it was the foundation of a business career," he recalls. "I was passionate about building a business, so it was a discipline I really needed to know in order to thrive and survive."

Of the challenging job market of today's young entrepreneurs, John advises an expansive and well-rounded repertoire of skills to remain competitive. "You've got to be everything—technically competent, good at interpersonal relationships, with strong written and oral communication skills and a constant drive to deliver your services more efficiently," he urges. He also details the fundamental importance of building a strong foundation in which you develop your core skills and perform an honest self-assessment to determine your ideal work path and work environments. "If you're honest with yourself about what you're good at and what you need to work on, you can thrive in an array of environments." John's advice stems not only from his own success, but also from applying his learn-by-example mentality to his own father. Amidst serving in World War II as well as raising and educating six children through professional programs, he maintained a lucrative career as a businessman and remained largely debt-free. The obstacles along our path may seem considerable, but John reminds us of the tremendous support we can derive from others, either through direct collaboration or through the indirect lessons we can learn from simply observing them. "Nobody does it on their own," he stresses. "Look for help, because it's there."

Keith Lemer

A Family History, a Family Future

Incredulous, the professor held a copy of *The Greek Telephone Directory* in his hands and then turned to its creator, a particularly ambitious student of his.

"You're the first person in my entrepreneurship class who actually took what we learned and applied it to the real world," he said.

At twenty-one years of age, Keith Lemer beamed. It wasn't the first time he had used an innovative idea to turn a profit, but it was certainly the most remarkable thus far. He had distinguished himself as an entrepreneur early in life, and whether he was selling t-shirts or employing the neighborhood kids to wash cars for him, the boy never seemed to run out of ideas. His college years at Syracuse University brought new successes with the institution of his coat check rental business, but the culmination of his young business career didn't come until the advent of his senior year when he founded a publishing business and began printing copies of the phone book his professor now held proudly in his hands.

The publication listed all the names and numbers of fraternity and sorority members on campus, along with pertinent advertisements from local businesses. After only two months' time, Keith had already generated $50 thousand with a fifty percent profit margin. He pursued this business after graduating, expanding the enterprise to 55 other colleges and universities across the country, living out of his car at times until he sold the company to an associate. Now the President of WellNet Healthcare, a medical management company founded in 1994, the innovation and strategy demonstrated throughout his early years foreshadowed the success he would facilitate in years to come.

If it's true that one has nothing without one's health, Keith Lemer makes it his business not only to ensure that we all having "something," but that we're maximizing that "something" as well. However, in order to fully understand WellNet's business model and impact, one must begin with a brief look at the statistics of the present day healthcare climate. When it comes to employer expenditures on health care, Keith points out that twenty percent of the workforce generally drives eighty percent of the costs, much of which result from ailments that are avoidable and manageable if detected early.

In the fifteen years since its inception, WellNet has undergone several different iterations that have enabled it to become what it is today. Originally founded by Harry Kovar, the business started out as a small pharmacy benefit management firm providing stand-alone prescription drugs for small and mid-size companies.

After *The Greek Telephone Directory*, Keith spent several years at a Private Equity firm in Los Angeles focused on sourcing healthcare and other bio-tech related investments from universities around the nation—companies developed by students and professors that needed seed capital to get their innovative ideas off the ground. This was a natural fit for Keith given his extensive prior experience working with universities across the country.

Itching to be participate in a venture in which he was able to control his own destiny, Keith joined Harry in 2000 after marrying Harry's daughter, Stephanie, and discussed WellNet's potential with his father-in-law in depth over many months. Though Stephanie and her mother discouraged the partnership for fear of business politics entering the family sphere, Keith and Harry were determined to move forward against everyone's wishes and developed an incredible working relationship, with Keith proving to be exactly what WellNet needed to take its next step. "I brought a different kind of entrepreneurship to the business," he remembers. The little company of three employees expanded to 55, and its revenue stream of $3 million escalated to $100 million in that timeframe.

Exactly how did this astounding growth come about? "We began to realize that the pharmacy data allowed us to see what was driving future medical costs today. This, in turn, allowed us to determine the appropriate strategies to put in place early on so companies would be able to avoid significant cost increases tomorrow," Keith explains. Seeing the potential in the concept, WellNet launched its own disease management division complete with nurses and care managers who could reach out to high and moderate risk patients identified with the pharmacy claim data, focusing on getting these patients healthy and compliant before the costs of those risks hit employer plans.

WellNet then evolved into its own administrator, paying claims and providing physician and facility network access to the same employer groups who were relying on insurance carriers that automatically raised their premiums 10 to 20 percent every year with little to no justification of such increases. Now a full-service medical management company providing pharmacy benefits, disease management, and third party administration to approximately 250 clients across the nation, WellNet's overall growth and staying power is a testament to the logic and innovation inherent in its design. "We've put mechanisms in place and worked on client and channel partner distribution relationships so that credible third-parties are selling—or rather educating—others on our approach, rather than WellNet promoting itself," Keith explains.

To expand this initiative even further, Keith and Harry joined forces with a technologist several years ago to design and implement Healthcare Interactive, a software development firm focused on building technologies that allow healthcare costs to be managed and measured online and in real time in much the same way corporations utilize CRM, ERP or Supply Chain Management software to manage and measure every other aspect of their business. Through the use of dashboards, workflows, predictive analytics, simulations, and member marketing campaigns, all integrated through a single environment, businesses are able to control and consolidate healthcare management on a single system, resulting in a 10 to 25 percent cost reduction. "Think Salesforce.com meets Facebook," says Keith.

"WellNet has thus built a technology solution that gives the control not to the insurance companies, and not to the brokers, but to the entity that's paying the bill—the CEO, the CFO, or the VP in Human Resources—so they can control health care expenses like any other aspect of their business," he continues.

One compelling aspect of this software is its incorporation of predictive modeling technology created by Johns Hopkins University, which creates a fingerprint of costs and risks through the context of a database of twenty million patients. Utilizing pharmacy data in this way provides extremely accurate insight and understanding into the high and moderate risk populations, allowing the plan sponsor to implement strategies and education programs in advance. In essence, it allows a corporation to build a custom program for each particular individual based on their disease states and risk stratification, thereby curbing risk before these individuals land in the hospital and incur medical expenses. Amidst a landscape where this kind of preventative forward thinking is otherwise nonexistent, WellNet equips employers with the insight, analytics and real-time action plan they need to make decisions that are best for both themselves and their employees.

Not only does WellNet provide avenues to create individualized and targeted care programs, but it also utilizes profiling to analyze a given population in order to ascertain the best way to communicate advice. "Once we pinpoint those key people, we engage them with strategies specific to their demographic and their issues," Keith explains. "This might be through text, chat, email, letters, or direct phone calls." This targeted program of outreach allows WellNet to boast an engagement rate of 40 to 80 percent, dramatically higher than the 5 to 10 percent engagement rates of traditional carriers.

The essence of WellNet, then, is elegantly simple. It takes a corporate discipline that is applied to every other aspect of business management and extends it into the healthcare realm. Not only does this allow employers to save money, but it translates into more savings and improved quality of life for employees as well. "Healthcare is a shared responsibility between the employer and employee, and it's in the best interest of all parties involved to take advantage of the data and engagement strategies," Keith emphasizes.

Considering the kind of vision and achievement-oriented focus required to run such an enterprise, it comes as no surprise that Keith hails from a large family of entrepreneurs. His father, for instance, created and owned Lemer Goldberg, once the largest Advertising Agency in Washington, D.C. He later sold it to purchase a radio station and ultimately honed in on shopping development, where he remains an active landlord today. Keith recalls how he was always buying and selling businesses, impassioned by the thrill of creating a business from scratch or one with tremendous potential and then selling the venture.

Likewise, his uncle owns The Bernstein Companies, one of Washington, D.C.'s oldest and premier real estate development and management organizations. This allowed him to gain seasoned insight into the political sphere, ultimately winning him the appointment of Ambassador to Denmark under George W. Bush. Yet another of Keith's uncles owns a government contracting firm, University Research Co., which focuses on healthcare and education in third-world countries. These three influences have been and continue to be pillars of guidance for Keith throughout his development.

"My father, uncle, cousins, and I all learn from each other, and we all draw from the life lessons of my grandfather, David Estrin, who spent 60 years of his life building, owning and operating District Wholesale," Keith reflects. The company supplied the inventory seen on the shelves of drugstore chains such as Dart-Drug, Drug-Fair, People's Drug and many other chain stores in the Mid-Atlantic. Mr. Estrin then sold the company to the conglomerate just 6 months before he passed away at the age of 81. The man had had an impeccable reputation, imbuing the family's bloodline with the entrepreneurial flare that fuels Keith today.

Despite this thorough rooting in an entrepreneurial history, however, Keith does not believe that a family tree of this nature is required to realize such success in business. "You can do anything you want to do as long as you put your mind to it," he insists. "Never settle. Gather as many experiences as you can to help inform the person you become." Keith's example does, however, suggest that it certainly helps to have a supportive and guiding infrastructure in place at an early age so one has the benefit of gathering these experiences and lessons from the start. "I knew from age four or five that I was going to work for myself," he remembers. "The idea was that, if you wanted to make a penny in this world, you had to get off your 'behind' to do it. For me, making money was not about *making* money, it was about not having to *worry* about money," he clarifies.

Just as Keith quickly acknowledges the role of family in his skills as an entrepreneur, he also readily explains how the concept of family becomes even more vital to success when applied to workplace relations. "Our nine main executives have played key roles in our growth," he explains. "We treat everyone like family here, and with that comes the family moral code of integrity—the idea that what you do and what you say are paramount in defining your character." For WellNet, success truly stems from the team behind the product and from Keith's firm commitment to the idea of leadership through collaboration.

Despite the ten years of growth and prosper that WellNet has already enjoyed, Keith feels that they've only just begun to hit their stride. In fact, he oftentimes feels as though the company is still in its fledgling stages. With so much under its belt already, WellNet's ability to identify opportunities and leverage its expertise to provide win-win-win situations inspires tremendous confidence.

Keith reminds us, however, that the motivation behind the mindset has always been and will always be family. "Money is only a way to keep score," he emphasizes. "People think building a company is about status, but that's the last thing that motivates me. The health and happiness of my family is all that matters. Everything I do, I do for them." With such a sustainable and infinite wellspring of motivation, it's no wonder WellNet has become the company it is today.

BERNHARDT

WEALTH MANAGEMENT

David Makarsky

The People behind the Profit

"I'm not going to take no for an answer," came the voice over the phone.

David Makarsky wasn't convinced, but his interest was piqued. The recent graduate and valedictorian of the Cornell Hotel School had received a number of exceptional job offers from many diverse walks of the industry, but he had decided to accept a position with Sheraton Hotels and Resorts. The company promised a very traditional experience, and David saw great value in beginning his post-graduate professional career with a firm foundation in formal training. Thus, he had to break the news to Rick Stottler, owner of a 300-seat restaurant on a pier in Cocoa Beach, Florida, that he wasn't interested in running the enterprise.

"At least come down and see it for yourself," Mr. Stottler urged.

David made the trek from upstate New York down to Cocoa Beach and again declined the offer, despite the charm and allure of the incredible waterfront asset. Insisting that he was giving up the opportunity of a lifetime, Mr. Stottler sweetened his offer one more time and then left the decision in David's hands. The young man considered the rarity of this unique dilemma, struck by the restaurant owner's words and persistence.

"You know what?" he said to himself. "Stop being so structured and inflexible. You're a young guy; you're twenty-one years old. Sheraton will always be there. You can fall flat on your face and still rebound."

David now considers his unconventional choice to accept the position of manager of the restaurant on Cocoa Beach Pier to be among the best decisions of his life. In the three and a half years he spent there, he developed a strong entrepreneurial spirit and a true sense of pride and ownership in his work that lent him an extraordinary and persistent inner drive. Even the most humbling of days—times in the early months of his employment when financial pressures were stifling and he wondered if he ever should have accepted the position—proved to be valuable learning experiences. He came to understand not only the value of offering an exceptional product through exceptional service, but also the value of developing solid and genuine relationships with staff, clients, vendors, and the surrounding community. David expanded upon the pier's original reputation as a tourist destination by transforming it into a community landmark, addressing the locals by name and celebrating their birthdays and anniversaries right along with them. With revenues increasing from $1 million during David's first year of management to $3.5 million at the time of his departure, it was truly a transformational time, both for the restaurant and for David himself.

Once he had accomplished what he could at the pier, he was approached by one of his regulars about working at Prime Hospitality, one of the larger hotel and management companies. At that time, Prime was building a new hotel in Cocoa Beach and courted him to become the opening Food and Beverage Director for the property. After working this job for a year, he also assumed management of a beachside diner that Prime had been struggling to implement successfully. "I would go to work in the morning at the hotel, work breakfast, get the banquets underway, and then I would be like Superman and change into a bowling shirt, black slacks, white socks, and penny loafers to run the diner," he remembers. Once his efforts paid off and the diner was successfully turned around, he was made Regional Director over fifteen hotels at the notable age of twenty-six.

During the seven years he worked at Prime and the subsequent six years he served at Servico Hotels and Resorts, he found himself traveling extensively. He and his wife had been forced to move their daughter, Danielle, five times within the first five years of her life, and with David traveling forty weeks a year, the young girl had begun to refer to the family telephone as "Daddy." Resolving to strike a healthier balance between the personal and professional spheres and to give his daughter an atmosphere of stability, he and his wife made one final move to the D.C. metropolitan area so he could assume a position with the B.F. Saul Company.

The roots of B.F. Saul can be traced back to 1851, when a renowned horticulturist by the name of John Saul was asked to relocate from his native Ireland to Washington, DC. Saul assumed the role of planning out the national parks on the Mall and its surrounding vicinity, and he purchased land in Montgomery County, Maryland, to grow the various shrubs and plants used in his work. His son, B. Francis Saul, took over after John's death, and in 1892 B.F. Saul began selling off parcels of the family land. He set up a mortgage company to finance the deals, and in the intervening years the business has evolved and diversified to become what it is today. The company currently focuses on a wide range of real estate considerations, including commercial property ownership, development, construction, management, leasing, and insurance.

The hotel division of B.F. Saul wasn't established until 1976, but it quickly flourished, currently owning and operating nineteen hotels in the D.C. metropolitan area. Eighteen of these are mid-market business class hotels like Marriots, Holiday Inns, and Hampton Inns. The nineteenth hotel, The Hay-Adams, is a luxury hotel located just down the street from the White House and has grown acclaim as the site where Barack Obama resided for the week preceding his inauguration.

David began his time at B.F Saul as a Regional Director of Operations, supervising five hotels and focusing on the tandem conversion of two hotels in Crystal City. The experience allowed him the balance he had been dreaming of, but he couldn't help but feel a sense of concern about some of his observations regarding the company's culture. One of the big draws of B.F. Saul had been its commitment to a set of core values that was referred to as Our Big Three. The company's mantra entailed a strong commitment to quality, both in its properties and in its team members, and David was instantly struck by the lighthearted yet genuine values embedded in its quality pledge. After actually working at B.F. Saul, however, he found that the words were inconsistently lent life through practice. Consequently, when the position of Vice President of Human Resources opened up, he immediately set his sights on the opportunity. "If we can succeed in developing a robust workplace culture," he explained to his manager, "it will pay big dividends in quality, in revenue, and in market share performance by developing repeat and referral business and by driving down turnover." His vision was inspiring, and he continued serving as Regional Director while also assuming the duties of Vice President of Human Resources. In this capacity he was able to instigate a structural reorganization that eventually resulted in a new position of Vice President of Operations, which he assumed and has been doing now for almost four years. The position has allowed him to maintain his first love of hotel operations while also pursuing his commitment to service and quality through the ultimate duty of fulfilling the company's mission statement—a role he refers to as "the greatest job in the world."

While David's current situation is inspiring in itself, it is lent even more potency in the context of his early life. Indeed, in choosing a career path, one oftentimes strives to emulate one's inner drive. The will to serve is a constant theme throughout David's life, first apparent at a very early age when he would lend a helping hand with siblings and other neighborhood children. Growing up in a very Leave-It-To-Beaver town, he recognized at an early age that his life was replete with blessings, and he always sought to give back to the community in thanks for his good fortune. He got very involved in his church and served as president of the youth group for two years, always supplementing his duties with community service work. David then pursued his will to serve through academics by focusing his studies on American Government throughout high school, envisioning a future career path in politics, public service, or law.

After he was accepted to the Arts and Sciences program at Cornell to major in Government, he knew he would have to contribute financially towards his education and assumed a work study position with Cornell Dining. What began as a job to fund his education and future career path instead became a new passion and a new vehicle through which David could exercise this inner drive to serve the community, and he found himself changing gears. By the end of his sophomore year, he had switched to Cornell's Hotel School and assumed a heavy workload that still enabled him to graduate within four years, setting him on the path that would eventually lead to the perfect job he now holds today.

His experience in school working for Cornell Dining was perhaps the best opportunity he could have hoped for, as it thoroughly immersed him in both the theory and the real world experience of the field. As a junior in college, he served as the Director of Catering and Special Events for the largest dining unit on campus, working forty to fifty hours per week on top of his course load. He maintained this back-breaking schedule throughout his senior year as well, assuming the position of Student Coordinator and managing all four hundred student workers. With fifteen supervisors and three managers reporting to him, the experience proved a valuable lesson in management and delegation and gave him much of the industry experience that warranted such high-powered job offers upon graduation.

"As I have grown and matured in my career, I have come to understand the power of people and just how important leadership is," says David. "As much as the technical side of business matters, success is ultimately defined by attracting talent to the organization and then engaging and retaining it." It is perhaps for this reason that he advises young people today to embrace the process of paying their dues as they enter the business world. In his industry, as with most, countless transactions take place in a day. Money, directions, and ideas are constantly exchanged from team members to guests, vendors, and other team members. A thorough understanding of these processes and how people are ultimately at the root of each transaction is the surest way to success and advancement. One must comprehend the varying dimensions at work in order to understand how to inspire the best in people, compelling them to put forth their optimal performance day in and day out.

Beyond understanding the mechanics of these transactions, however, David's success can ultimately be traced back to an unrelenting and genuine passion for service and people. It is evident in the personalized notes in the birthday and employment anniversary cards he sends to each of the 180 managers in the hotel division each year. It is evident in the periodic events and projects he plans to promote team member pride and unity, and it is evident in the steady decline of the division's turnover rate from 77% to 28% since his involvement with HR. "It's the glue that binds a thousand team members across eighteen hotels regardless of the brand they're affiliated with," he says of B.F. Saul's quality pledge. Perhaps this "glue" really is the statement, or perhaps it's David himself.

Basim Mansour

The Constant Runner

Above all else, Basim Mansour is a runner. Not a track runner, not a trail runner, but a *life* runner.

While the cement of this disposition was poured long ago, it wasn't until his beloved father's untimely death of a heart attack in 1990 that the solidification was complete. Mousa "Michael" Basim had been the hardworking founder of Michael & Son, a full-service electric company, and as Proud Son in the equation, nineteen-year-old Basim shouldered the burden of running the company without a single word of protest. "It was very important to me not to cry at his viewing and funeral," Basim remembers. "I wanted to be strong for my mother and sister. The most important thing to me after that was getting back into the office and moving forward. I wanted to start running." And so Basim did just that, sprinting through the 1990 recession, through his own learning curve, and through the struggles that followed.

One night after a particularly vigorous day, he found himself in his car with a pounding headache, his mind flooded with such a slew of worries over paying bills and managing the company that he could hardly think straight. And yet suddenly, the young man's mind sharpened into a crystal-clear recognition. "I realized that my problems weren't going to kill me, so what?" he recalls. As soon as he came to this understanding and told himself to let go, the stress and headache dissipated and he stood peaceful and calm in the face of the storm. "Maintaining this calm in thinking helps me get things done better," he says now.

In the intervening years since that night, this sense of calm and quiet strength has become as much a part of Basim's character as the urge to run, resulting in a compelling mix of traits that at first seem contradictory but are rather inherently intertwined. In truth, his ascension up the ladder toward betterment isn't some jittery, haphazard climb—rather, it is a purposeful, steady, reliable drive. "Life is lived on a treadmill, and the moment you stop running is the moment you're going backwards," he says. "To quit growing is to stop living, so I'll be running as long as God lets me." The urgency in his step inspires others to do the same, and it is with this still and steadfast passion that he has led Michael & Son down the path to success thus far.

The company was first launched in 1976 by Mousa Mansour, an electrician who did commercial and residential electric and construction work. Compelled by a strong sense of familial duty, Basim began working with his father at the age of five. "I was always sensitive to my parents and my surroundings," he remembers. "When I knew that my family was struggling, I just felt it was my duty and my job to do what I could to help." After managing Michael and Son during the day, Basim's father would work nights at the Hyatt Regency Hotel as an engineer. The family also owned a restaurant where his mother worked a full day until seven o'clock at night, after which she would return home to sleep for a few hours and rise in time to work her shift at a Toddle House breakfast restaurant from midnight until six in the morning. "You'd have to be a real non-caring, non-feeling person to see that kind of thing and not do what you had to do to help," he says. To contribute, Basim got a job working a paper route at age eleven, rising at four in the morning to deliver papers to his neighborhood and $150 per month to his family's resources. He kept none of the money for himself.

Aside from the paper route, working for Michael & Son was the only job Basim ever had, and he developed the skills of his craft so proficiently that he was serving as lead electrician for ten thousand square foot projects by the age of sixteen. He studied with Mousa every summer, every weekend, and even after school when time permitted. When the young man was seventeen, his father received a large promotion job to replace twelve thousand lights in a nearby high school, and Basim ran the job on his own. Then, when Mousa's ability to train his son in the trade came to its abrupt and tragic halt, Basim dropped out of college to take over the business—a one-truck operation with one or two employees at the time.

With so much yet to learn about managing the company, he completed the contracts his father had taken on before his death and then refined the company's repertoire to solely electrical work, hoping to start afresh with an element of organization that had been otherwise lacking in Michael & Son. Then, in 1999, the company assumed service work, adding a construction and handyman component to which Basim had always been naturally drawn. With the new business model, his fleet of trucks expanded to three. Plumbing was later added in 2004, followed by HVAC in 2008. "The reality is that if you're truly a service business, you want to take care of the customer," Basim remarks. "The genesis of our diversification served to make the customer's life easier—for example, allowing us to patch up drywall after electrical work."

The company's growth in the intervening years has been nothing short of exponential. "Less than ten years ago, we were operating out of my garage, with the shop on the second floor and the office on the first," Basim reports. When they purchased their first condo warehouse, he remembers how the unit's sheer size reminded him of a Costco. Contrary to the advice of his manager and sister, he soon bought two neighboring warehouses to supplement the first, which the company eventually outgrew. They added another building and then yet another, expanding their parking lots out over the land to accommodate the influx of employees. Now a complete electrical, plumbing, HVAC, construction, and handyman operation, Michael & Son services everywhere from Baltimore to Winchester to Fredericksburg and extending down to Richmond, Norfolk, and Virginia Beach. Today, the company has over 150 trucks and about 220 employees, drawing $40 million in revenue this year alone.

When it comes to the future of Michael & Son, Basim isn't hesitating to shoot for the moon. He expects the company's revenues to mirror the impressive growth they've seen recently, predicting that its size will double in the next three years. "I want to be a hundred million dollar service company," he says, and then pauses. "Then I want to be a billion dollar service company!" Growth is expected to be accomplished in part through franchising, which Basim is working on currently. He envisions the sweeping of his brand across the U.S., making Michael & Son a household name. Once he gets to that point, he expects his goal will then be to extend internationally. "I know myself," he says. "I know that once we reach our goals in the states, I'll continue to ask myself what comes next."

To this effect, it's interesting to note that Basim works not because he has to, but because this sense of perpetual forward motion runs deep in his veins. He doesn't even use an alarm clock—rather, his life and work flow, enmesh, and perpetuate incredibly organically. "A job represents some place you have to be in order to make money, but a business is a part of your very existence that brings you money incidentally," Basim explains. "A lot of business owners have jobs, but I don't.

I have a business." Through his business, Basim is able to facilitate the kind of deep connections that bring life its greater worth. This is accomplished in one sense through the relationship Michael and Son cultivates with the community. Their website, for instance, emanates a personality, sincerity, and amity that is lacking in many larger corporations today. Philanthropy is another important component in the company's relationship to the community, not to mention the generation-spanning connection between Michael and Basim, which Basim hopes will be continued through one of his own sons. "You have to be part of the world, part of the nation, part of the community. There's no such thing as a single-souled person in this world," he confirms.

When it comes to advising young people entering the workforce today, Basim employs the KISS acronym, representing the humorous yet compelling idea to "keep it simple, stupid." He applies this philosophy to a string of succinct yet powerful phrases for further instruction. "Make a plan. Set a goal. Bust your ass," he says. "Don't try to do too much, but instead master a few skills really well. Wait until your business has built a foundation of success before branching out into other services." Positioning one's self as an expert in a single matter is paramount to success, and in this sense, knowledge is power. "If you want to run a show, you've got to *be* the show. You've got to know more than anyone else about the topic at hand," he emphasizes, echoing his father's sentiments exactly.

Beyond this advice, Basim leads by example: a port in the storm, a runner moving steadily toward success, and a family man with unshakable integrity and work ethic. An old-fashioned man at heart, he's the kind of guy who loves to guarantee trust and sincerity through a simple handshake. "I strive to always walk—or run, rather—on the ground," says Basim.

In his further attempts to delineate a picture of what it means to be truly successful, Basim recalls the glossy pages of a particular issue of Time magazine featuring a relatively early photograph of famed boxer

Mike Tyson. Basim recalls being instantly captivated by the photo, which portrayed an exhausted yet perseverant Tyson in the moments following a particularly grueling workout. "In order to succeed, it is not good enough to say you're doing your best. In order to succeed, you must do what is necessary," says Basim, quoting Winston Churchill. Tyson's posture epitomizes these words as he sprawls in the photograph, sweat-stained and dog-tired, recuperating after throwing his last ounce of strength and stamina into the workout.

"There's a lot of satisfaction in giving everything you've got, and the biggest regret in a lot of peoples' lives is not being the best person they could have been or doing the best job they could have done," says Basim. This means perpetually redefining your limits, reconfiguring your mind in terms of what is possible and impossible. It means to start and finish your race with the kind of quiet strength that allows one to persevere—a resolve that comes not from without, but within. Ready, set, go.

Dario Marquez

The Strategist's Perspective

Aboard the plane home after a notably demanding mission in Honduras, Dario Marquez couldn't stop thinking about a particular passage from Jay Levinson's *Guerrilla Marketing*. "If you can't predict your sales in the future, you're a ship without a rudder," he recalled to himself. His mission critical services company, MVM Inc., was founded in 1979 and had experienced considerable growth in the ten years since, developing an impressive client list that included the Rockefeller family, Henry Kissinger, Kellogg, Time Magazine, and several wealthy clients from Saudi Arabia, Qatar, and Kuwait. Since leaving the secret service after ten years of employment and joining forces with two other former agents to create MVM, their incremental success was a testament to their industry experience and unique perspective on executive protection. Dario, however, feared the company was at a standstill, and could not help but ruminate on the stagnation as the plane gained altitude.

On this flight that some would call serendipitous and others would call fate, Dario happened to mention his apprehension to a fellow passenger who suggested he target government contracts, pointing out that the U.S. government is the largest procurer of security services in the world. It was a time of political tension—Reagan had just come into office, the Iranian hostage crisis still hung in the air, and Bobby Inman had just been commissioned to do a study on the security of individuals working in Foreign Service. His research culminated in the Omnibus Diplomatic Security Anti-Terrorist Act of 1986 and proclaimed that American embassies were victims of terror, ill-prepared to deal with potential threats. This prediction was rendered a painful reality when U.S. officials discovered that the Moscow embassy had been built by the KGB and was riddled with bugs. A contract to protect the embassy was open for bids in 1987, and because of Dario's conversation on the airplane, MVM won.

Launching the company into a heightened domain of competitive edge, MVM went from revenues of $400,000 one year to $10 million the next. Always the forward thinker, however, Dario's previous fears dissipated just as new ones took shape. With one contract in the bag and the company expanding to meet its needs, he noted that all the eggs were essentially in one basket. Thus, diversification became the theme and lifeblood of MVM, with four major divisions eventually taking shape: security, professional services, global support services, and a training facility.

With diversification largely completed, MVM is now primarily concerned with the two goals which Dario terms "transformation" and "transition". The transformation he refers to is the effort to develop the professional services, global support services, and training facility divisions of the company, aiming to elevate them to the strength that their security program already possesses. In terms of transition, Dario and his staff are training his son, Kevin, to serve as his successor as chief executive officer and president. Acutely aware that many family-owned businesses fail in the face of the discontinuity and disarray bred from the passing of the torch to the second generation, Dario is facing this challenge with the same strategic superthinking he applies to other areas of business. He describes the process as "a constant conversation"—everyone is involved and encouraged to give feedback, and the team is committed to an orderly and systematized process in which the expectations of all parties are streamlined through communication.

Now, several decades after the fortuitous conversation on the plane from Honduras, MVM has exploded into a $200 million company, aiming to reach $500 million within the next five years. Despite its rapid expansion, Dario and his family have made a concerted effort to maintain a genuine compassion and connection with MVM's 3,000 workers, keeping the human aspects of management in focus. His late wife, Karen, had started a tradition of sending a card to each staff member on their birthday, and the practice which has become integral to the company's identity. Dario also attributes this management philosophy to Mary Furlow, a mentor who had served as his supervisor earlier in his career. She exhibited a tremendous sense of empathy but, at the same time, didn't hesitate to make the tough decisions that life sometimes requires. Her direct nature and charisma were fueled by a courage of conviction that Dario strives to emulate as a leader today.

Just as seminal as his relational skills, however, is Dario's impact as a strategist and long-term planner. Truly effective strategy requires 360-degree vision, and this is what Dario has aimed to deliver from day one. One might argue that he began building this vision during his first high school job working as a cook's helper in a state-owned senior citizen's facility near Morristown, New Jersey. Says Dario of the experience, "It showed me what I *didn't* want." Equipping him with a strong drive for success that fit well with the incredible work ethic inspired by his mother, he attended Southeastern University at night while supporting a wife and children at the same time.

The most integral aspects of his education, however, were gained during the ten years he served as a secret service agent. It was during this time that he acquired the tools to both broaden and hone his vision, gaining exhaustive expertise in executive protection, a very specialized area of law enforcement. When faced with the prospect of leaving the service to start his own company, he considered his options in the strategic manner that has become his hallmark. Could he picture himself content with his boss's job? What about his boss's boss's job? What about as the director of secret service? When the answer to each question was in the negative, he directed his attention to several of the entrepreneurs his work brought him in contact with. His admiration for their very individual accomplishments was undeniable, and he noted that he was still young enough to find another job if he attempted a venture and failed. His wife provided exceptional encouragement, and the voice of his mother's entrepreneurial spirit compelled him onward. She had always dreamed of owning her own business, and the example of her tenacity inspired Dario to pursue his own dream—among the best decisions of his life.

Despite such positive support, however, it is unlikely that Dario's venture would have proven so successful if not for his strategic personality. In addition to the 360-degree vision that allows one to identify past trends and predict future pitfalls, his position as a leader and innovator relies upon his capacity to ask the right questions. What are the threats and opportunities inherent in a given situation? Are we prepared to capture the opportunities as they present themselves? To Dario, working is like a big chess game in which one must carefully analyze and envisage the moves of one's own team and one's competition.

It is interesting to note that this process of strategizing draws heavily on a keen perception of the world around you. Without the assistance of scientific and technical research aimed at predicting the future, Dario and his colleagues were able to plot their moves by making detailed inferences in light of the current political and technical climates. One must also note that mistakes should not unravel an agenda, but should rather be utilized as valuable learning tools. As Dario points out, human beings learn far more from their mistakes than they do from their successes. This system of learning from experience is formalized and optimized through business coaching programs in which executives can learn from their peers and from keynote speakers from all disciplines and backgrounds. Dario participated in one such specialized coaching program, Vistage, which provided him with invaluable learning opportunities and is an experience he would recommend to any young entrepreneur today.

One other valuable piece of advice he offers is his perspective on how a successful strategist treats reality. While the truth can sometimes engender anxiety and unrest, it should always be viewed as an ally instead of an adversary. Maintaining a clear and informed conception of the world around him helps Dario to operate under reasonable and conservative constraints that would safeguard MVM if a given worst case scenario ever came to fruition. Though the coming years look prosperous for the company, with a number of acquisitions in sight that could provide the transformative force necessary to change MVM from a federal security support company to a full-fledged professional services enterprise, it is certainly prepared to weather storms along the way if necessary.

As MVM now prepares Dario's son, Kevin, to assume more and more responsibility, Dario himself is looking to the future. He's currently taking flying lessons and eagerly anticipates the earning of his pilot's license—an almost metaphorical expression of his work toward the success of MVM. "I think my role, which I enjoy doing, is to look out over the horizon and say, there's many ways we could go, but we're going in that direction," he explains. Communicate your vision in strategic detail—how it will be accomplished, why you need others to follow your lead, what the outcome will look like—and people will be moved by that vision. When one pictures the former secret service agent flying his single-engine high above the clouds, one recalls the plane flight home from Honduras that helped to shape his vision. One considers the many times throughout MVM's development in which he was able to see above the clouds to lead his company toward success, and one can only wonder about what opportunities the organization will seize down the road.

Robert Morgan

The Infused Workplace

Bob Morgan lifted his first bail of hay at age twelve. Though he had a lot to learn about dairy farming on that small plot of land in rural Pennsylvania, his grandfather was always thankful for the help and never failed to put the boy to work. Years later now, Bob reflects back on his grandfather's love of the farm when the old man offered him the opportunity to take it over. The thought of continuing his legacy was admirable, and yet Bob sensed his calling guiding him in a different direction.

"It's yours if you want it, but if you're not passionate about it, you should continue on and get your degree," his grandfather urged. "This was my dream, but it may not be yours!"

Though Bob has long since left those days on the dairy farm behind him, he keeps the passion and positivity of his grandfather's words alive in the work he does every day. Now the Co-Founder and Chief

Executive Officer of a business and technology solutions company called MorganFranklin, he believes this passion allows for a kind of positive energy in the workplace for which there is no substitute. "It's about waking up in the morning and being energized about what you do," he emphasizes. "You should also surround yourself with others who have positive energy because it builds on itself."

Much of the vigor in this positive energy draws from a deep sense of pride and enthusiasm about what MorganFranklin does. With approximately sixty percent of their contracts in government, employees are able to serve in high-intensity environments on national security issues and enjoy a sense of honor in keeping the country safe. With the other forty percent of contracts in the commercial sector, they are also challenged to solve high-stakes problems for large and complicated publicly-traded companies. MorganFranklin also boasts a vast geographical reach, with employees in ten to fifteen countries throughout the world, not to mention Florida, Chicago, Texas, California, Ohio, South Carolina, New York, Virginia, and Maryland. This international presence opens new avenues of opportunity for employees, and the company's government and business development team is leveraging this breadth to bid on much larger contracts.

The concept of MorganFranklin was first seeded in 1998 when Bob Morgan and Rob Franklin, then employees for a government engineering program, decided to strike out on their own. At that time, they were managing their own programs and enjoyed the freedom to create there own business space. With both of them working towards their MBAs and getting the sense that their progress in Federal Government had reached a plateau, their restlessness was compounded by a recent shift in one of their major programs. With that, the "light bulb" went off, inspiring them to take the ultimate risk. Aiming to draw upon the best of what they'd seen in the government contracting realm, they teamed up with Bob's brother, CPA and fellow entrepreneur Ron Morgan, and founded a government contracting company that upheld their own culture, philosophy, and ideals.

While they originally intended to be a systems integrator company, they abandoned their business plan within the first year. Recognizing the need in most organizations, both government and commercial, for assistance with finance, accounting, operations, and management technology, they sought to fill this need. Now they offer a full range of strikingly diverse services, including business, finance, and management consulting. Systems engineering integration work is also included in their repertoire.

One of the major inflection points in the company's history came in 2003, when they realized they were using their newfound growth to chase every opportunity they saw, which in turn left them vulnerable and undiscerning. The success of the enterprise suffered, and they found themselves in a defining moment. Seizing the opportunity, they reigned in their forces and focused on retrenching, identifying their fortes and capitalizing rather than spreading resources too thin. With this narrowing of focus, they saw explosive growth in core areas through the next several years. This is a technique they still employ today, restricting any new service offerings to focus on their core strengths.

Another key era for MorganFranklin's development was, surprisingly, the recession. "It was a bit of a slap in the face," Bob muses, "but we came out of it with a much leaner and more efficient workforce. It gave us a chance to reflect and reconfirm our commitment to a performance-based mentality." Now, with more than $50 million in revenue, the company aims to grow 15-20% each year over the next three years, supplementing its organic expansion with strategic acquisitions currently in the works. And, through the implementation of business development processes including improved financing and accounting systems and new incentive compensation programs, Bob is confident that MorganFranklin's well-placed infrastructure and achieved maturity will assimilate this projected growth in stride.

Despite the company's tremendous expansion and profitability, one might be surprised to learn that Bob measures his success on a different scale. "Growth awards are nothing compared to awards of workplace excellence," he divulges. As the winner of numerous recognitions for workplace excellence, flexibility, balance, and health consciousness, it comes as no surprise that departing employees often refer to Morgan-Franklin as the best place they'd ever worked. This is a testament to Bob's leadership philosophy, which emphasized a deep and nuanced understanding of his employees' needs, both professionally and personally. "Managing is directing," he explains, "but leadership is knowing what motivates your workers and what they're going through that might impact their performance." Employees are routinely given one-on-one attention by the leadership team and receive regular updates about the state of the company through what Bob describes as "town hall meetings." And if an employee ever just wants to pop in and say hello, Bob and his leadership team maintain an open door policy.

This leadership style manages to promote a focused work ethic while still maintaining the balance between work and non-work life that Bob feels to be so essential—a perspective that takes root in a series of experiences he had many years ago. They commenced the summer before his sophomore year of college, when he first received the diagnosis that would change him forever: cancer. After surgery to remove the tumor, the cancer abated briefly but returned two years later, launching him through a chemotherapy regimen that "officially" cured him. Soon after that, however, the doctors discovered another grapefruit-sized tumor in his lower back. Emotionally exhausted and worn through by the rollercoaster of the past several years, he withstood one final surgery and bout of chemo.

In retrospect, Bob reflects on the tremendous respect he has developed over the years for the physicians that charted the course to his eventual recovery. Though his chief doctor was the nation's third best physician specializing in that specific kind of cancer and an expert in his own right, the physician didn't hesitate to ask the advice and opinions of other doctors to supplement his own knowledge. "This has had a *huge* impact on how I approach problems, issues, and conflicts," he confirms. "I like to soak in all the information before making any kind of decision or judgment. There are three sides to every story." Beyond this, he strives to worry only about what he can control. With the births of his three "miracle" sons even after he had been told the chemotherapy would prevent him from ever having children, Bob has living proof that the uncontrollable aspects of life can work themselves out in the end.

MorganFranklin is thus infused with the riveting life lessons Bob has picked up over the years. This is not to imply, however, that the softer side of its company culture is not balanced with unequivocal structure and rational rigidity. "We're not a lifestyle business," Bob explains. "We've made it clear that we want to grow." Opportunity and positivity are the centerpieces of the work environment at MorganFranklin, allowing this propensity for growth to reflect in each of its 300 employees. The culture promotes a healthy work/life balance while also striving to reward those that put in the extra effort. The opportunities to grow, evolve, and advance are plentiful, but each employee is ultimately responsible for their own professional development. As Bob describes, "Each new employee is told that they will make mistakes, and it is how they respond to these mistakes that matters. Do they take accountability? Do they collaborate and try to resolve?" To Bob, coping style and accountability are the key to success—not only at MorganFranklin, but in life.

In this sense, Bob would advise young entrepreneurs to achieve the kind of scalability in their ideals that he strives to achieve in MorganFranklin. Just as the company as a whole is now competing in a global market, each individual entering the workforce today must seek to define themselves in a market that is broad, competitive, and complex. Though there are blueprints and guidelines for scaling systems, policies, and procedures, the company culture that sets MorganFranklin apart is harder to translate, and this is the task set forth for Bob now. In a similar manner, he instructs, "Create your own belief system and then apply this to wherever you work, and don't be afraid to accept your lowest-paid opportunity if it gives you the greatest chance to grow in the future." By seizing your opportunities and not being afraid to infuse your work with the culture and positive energy you believe in, young entrepreneurs might one day build a company with the kind of vitality and zest that emanates from MorganFranklin.

Gary Nakamoto

A Passion for Compassion

Despite his obvious success and considerable impact, it doesn't take one long to figure out that Gary Nakamoto isn't from around here. Exuding a humbleness and congeniality that is as inspiring as it is genuine, one wonders where these traits—rare in the competitive world of business—find their roots. "We lived all over the place," he laughs now, recalling his somewhat nomadic childhood. After his parents' divorce when he was five years old, his mother moved the small family around the Midwest as they struggled to make ends meet. Gary himself participated in a wide range of activities to help contribute—mowing lawns, collecting soda bottles by the highway, washing dishes, bussing tables, digging ditches, assisting with farming, and working in sewage and septic cleaning, to name a few.

Now the Chairman of Base Technologies, Inc, of the Washington, D.C. Metro Area, it is clear that this compassion and kindness are built on a solid and unswerving interior. "This is the strength of our beginnings," he remarks. "I am considerate to everyone, but when push comes to shove, I stand up. You don't get to where you want to go by sitting down, that's for sure."

Gary's childhood developed this particularly strong sense of universal and nondiscriminatory respect in his character that continues to factor strongly into his leadership philosophy today. "I never look down on anyone now because there is hardly any odd job I haven't done myself," he remarks. "I always appreciate everyone, and this is the kind of wisdom and attitude I now hope to instill in my own son." This sense of kindness is preceded by a true openness of spirit to people, ideas, and opportunities that has helped to lead him where he is now. "I don't believe that people should have just an open door policy," Gary confirms. "I want to know that people have an open *mind* policy."

This unique spin on a common phrase demonstrates the style of leadership that Gary has honed throughout his life—a life that has been far from typical, and that has in turn bred a far from typical strength of character. After the frequent moves of his early years, Gary's family settled in Meigs County in Appalachia by the time he was entering fifth grade. He barely graduated from the county's high school, known by his peers as a class clown. "I was good in athletics but would probably have been voted Least Likely to Succeed," he remembers. Though he trailed academically toward the bottom of his graduating class of 140 students, he continued on to school at Ohio University where he did well and concentrated in management studies.

Upon receiving his degree in 1988, he promptly relocated to Washington, DC where began studying for his Series 7 license. "I learned that you have to take who you are and try to mold who you want to become," says Gary. To make a living during this interim, he accepted a friend's invitation to become a car salesman, where he made a good paycheck and earned himself the title of top seller within his first month of employment. His ascension dealership manager was swift and certain, and he remained in the auto industry until his father, Bob Nakamoto, hired him on at Base Technologies. "It was a gamble for my dad to do this, but he's an entrepreneur at heart," Gary observes. "He saw my people and leadership skills combined with the ability to train and cope with considerably adverse conditions, as the auto industry comes with particularly rough terrain."

Bob had originally founded Base Technologies in 1987. Drawing on his extensive experience in Federal and state government working in large-scale computer systems, the company specialized in consulting of this nature for the first five years of its existence. When Gary stepped onto the scene in 1997, it had just begun to pursue a blend of public and private sector involvement. In essence, Base Technologies now operates systems through its expertise in network engineering, systems engineering, web application development, and the management of large infrastructures. They manage one of the largest data centers in the world and are thus extremely well-versed in complex, high-end IT work, serving clients like IBM and Fujitsu. Their competency also spans a vast array of products and integration technology. Notable assignments include the Atlanta Clean Air campaign and the production of driver's licenses for the Commonwealth of Virginia.

When Gary first started with Base Technologies, he was hired for a position in business development, working to brand the company's identity in the marketplace and supporting whatever needed to be done to grow. "When I started, I saw tremendous untapped potential," he recalls. "The company resembled a lot of unplowed, unused land. I knew that if I was willing to get up early and work hard all day, I had a chance to make something incredible." He then moved on to a higher-level management position until he became CEO in 2002. His father knew he had always had strong people skills and cared deeply about anything he committed to, so it seemed natural to pass the family business on to Gary.

After further developing the company for several years as CEO, Gary then promoted a member of his staff into that position and himself transitioned on as Chairman. "I now see my role as a supporter in whatever area the current CEO requires assistance with, whether it's operations, infrastructure, business development, or protocol improvement," Gary explains. This keen insight into skill and role management is one key character trait that has allowed the company to thrive under Gary's leadership rather than wilt as so many second-generation family businesses are apt to do.

"What makes this place different, and what I'm really proud of, are the people who work here," Gary continues. "Our leadership and management team expects not only ethical behavior, but a genuine passion and personal investment in the work that we do and the opinions of co-workers, clients, and partners." For Gary, a wealth of successful experience is only as good as the attitude and enthusiasm behind it, which should persist even if a project faces unanticipated obstacles or frustrations. Participating in a highly competitive industry in an equally competitive geographic region where everyone is an expert, the people beyond the paper are what ultimately make the difference. "Clients want to be able to see and trust the person that's going to be working on their site," he acknowledges.

Today, Base Technologies maintains an impressive track record of stability and boasts a commitment to growth despite tremendous economic upheavals. It currently employs slightly over two hundred people clustered primarily in the Mid-Atlantic region of the U.S. but also spanning the globe, supporting military technologies in Afghanistan, Iraq, and Kuwait. The company draws $45 million in revenue and expects to maintain a trend of growth in the years to come.

Surprisingly, however, Gary does not advocate a five-year plan but instead urges one to be lithe and prepared to take the utmost advantage of any opportunity that might arise. "Every five-year plan is not worth the paper it's written on," he explains. "Take 9/11 and the two major market meltdowns we've had this decade. What five-year plan has survived these? Instead, every business must be prepared, fit, and ready to fight like hell to win. Nobody can predict the future, so you must be prepared to expand your mind beyond what you *thought* the game would look like." In this sense, one must be able to wake up each morning with a good plan and be willing to adjust it throughout the day. "These are very fluid times we live in," Gary confirms.

Beyond the maintenance of this ready-to-spring posture, Gary's most urgent piece of advice to young entrepreneurs today is a simple moral trait he learned from observing the most influential person in his life, his mother: compassion. "No matter what you're doing, have compassion for others and never have an exaggerated sense of self-importance," he suggests. "It's not about you, it's about everyone." This sense of compassion is tied closely to responsibility and trust, which bundle together to create a strong team spirit that is at once enlivening and self-sustaining. "If someone fumbles the ball, don't waste time pointing fingers. Just jump on it!" he implores. "This kind of trust and teamwork goes a long way in life, whether you're in combat, on a sports team, or in a relationship."

As a gesture of the compassion he so fiercely advocates, Gary invites a group of high school students from Meig County to come to the Washington, D.C. Metro Area each summer to get a taste of the nation's capital while seeing how entrepreneurship works through Base Technologies. "I enjoy hearing about the students and their families, and I enjoy the opportunity to expose them to something different," he explains. "It would have been a game changer for me had I had that kind of exposure when I was in high school, so it's important for me to pass the opportunity on to others."

The relevance this current act of philanthropy has in the context of Gary's personal history echoes the significance Gary places on a more broadly scoped history in the evolution of his management style. In particular, he looks to Abraham Lincoln as a compelling character after which his own philosophy is modeled. "Lincoln was a poor farmer with no education and could have just as easily stayed in the wilderness," explains Gary, mirroring his own beginnings in many ways. "Instead, he looked at the world and related himself to it, which made him brilliant," he marvels. "No book teaches you how to look at a situation and figure out how you can make it better—to do this, you must look into yourself." Just as Gary has built a stronger company through employing such principles, humor, humility, and follow-through, so can each individual strengthen and elevate their lot by embracing similar tenets of character and tenacity.

Bonnie Phipps

The Power of Education

Sometimes, the best stories begin with a single decision—the kind of decision that, in retrospect, changes everything. Bonnie Phipps, for instance, could have just as easily decided not to go back to school. Having dropped out of college at the University of Maryland after her freshman year and moved down to Atlanta, life seemed pretty good as it was at the time. She was making decent money, so the decision to obtain her degree was not made out of necessity, nor would the task be a quick or painless endeavor. Regardless, after six years of experience in the working world, she enrolled at Georgia State for night school and spent the next six years working toward her undergraduate degree. She then worked another five years to obtain her masters. Now the President and CEO of St. Agnes Healthcare Inc., the effort she expended throughout this extensive tenure has since made all the difference in the world.

Bonnie had always liked hospitals. As a young girl, she would tag along with her mother during her routine volunteering at Maryland General Hospital and would herself work as a candy striper. It was quite fitting, then, when she later got a job as a controller at a hospital while slowly but surely plowing her way through school. While working at a variety of acute care hospitals in the Atlanta area, she got her BBA with suma cum laude honors and was subsequently promoted to CFO as she worked toward her MPA degree. Her husband then challenged her to get her CPA. "You'll never be more ready to earn it than you are now," he had urged. "If you wait, you'll just have to re-learn everything all over again later on."

"When I first arrived in Atlanta in the early seventies, I really had the feeling that I could make it without an education," Bonnie recalls. "Now, looking back, getting an education was like getting my tickets punched, and it made the biggest difference because it qualified me to do anything I wanted to do." Though she originally went to school thinking she would teach accounting, she soon came to the realization that her true passion lay right where she had spent the entirety of her working career—in healthcare. Experience and expansion then became the name of her game, and she asked her boss to extend her responsibilities into the countless specialized departments of the hospital—"departments like cardiology and gastroenterology and just about any other-ology you can think of," Bonnie laughs now. "It was then that I decided I wanted to be a CEO." This goal was first realized in 1996 while she was still in Atlanta, paving the way for her future at St. Agnes as their first woman non-Sister CEO.

As a woman in a male-dominated field, Bonnie was somewhat of a hot commodity and had attracted the attention of several recruiters interested in diverse candidates. With a husband who flew for Delta Airlines, Bonnie considered herself fairly tethered to Atlanta until his retirement. When she received the call about the open position for St. Agnes, however, her interest was piqued. Bonnie's background in

Catholic healthcare and her experience working in high-end specialized, teaching-oriented, and Magnet-certified hospitals rendered her an ideal candidate. Furthermore, St. Agnes had reached a point where there was work to be done in rebuilding relationships with medical staff—the kind of feat where Bonnie's unique expertise would truly have an opportunity to shine. In every way, it seemed like a match made in heaven, and after a rigorous four-month interview process, she accepted the position.

Currently clocking in at 148 years of service, St. Agnes was established by the Daughters of Charity as Baltimore's first Catholic hospital. It maintains 332 beds and 25,000 admissions per year in addition to seeing 110,000 patients. 85,000 of these patients are seen in the hospital's emergency department, making it the second largest emergency department in Baltimore. All of this is accomplished with 3,100 employees and a medical staff of eight hundred. St. Agnes also has a sister hospital, called Providence, in Washington, DC. Its charter, only one year older than that of St. Agnes, was signed by Abraham Lincoln.

St. Agnes is still sponsored by the Daughters of Charity and is part of Ascension Health, the largest Catholic system in the country. Bonnie appreciates the inspirational yet respectful spiritual overlay lent to the hospital by its Catholic roots. The Sisters, for instance, will diplomatically call for a moment of silence before meetings to reflect upon the meaning and good fortune of their ability to be present. In truth, Bonnie could have opted to work for a Big Eight accounting firm like Arthur Andersen. Such a route would have earned her a considerably higher salary, at least at the outset. Despite this knowledge, however, her path remained steadfast. "I love working in healthcare and working with doctors," she explains. "I love how intelligent they are and how I am still challenged by the medical community everyday." Unlike most other hospital CEOs, Bonnie demonstrates a genuine passion for the medical field and surprises her doctors by attending the staff education meetings whenever she can.

Though the typical tenure for a hospital CEO is about five years, Bonnie has already spent four and a half at St. Agnes and has just extended her commitment for several more years at least. She also serves as the Ministry Market Leader for Ascension Health with responsibilities for the hospitals and nursing homes that comprise the organization's Mid-Atlantic presence. Thus, Bonnie's days remain as vast and varied as they are long. Aside from overseeing a multi-million dollar construction project that will transform the hospital's campus, for instance, she spends about twenty-five percent of her time performing duties for the rest of her Ascension Health market. This includes board meetings in DC, board and finance committee meetings for her ministries, and meeting other industry market leaders monthly in St. Louis to discuss System activities.

When she's not meeting with physicians or her VP teams to discuss St. Agnes's daily considerations, she might be meeting with potential donors to promote the Capital campaign or interviewing potential board members. Because hospitals are unique in that they're a 24/7 operation, it is commonplace for Bonnie to work a twelve-hour day. Still, she feels that the vast majority of the hospital CEOs she knows love what they do. With such an honest and intelligent work environment focused around such a positive and compelling mission, this is not hard to believe. "Yes, I could have opted for a job that paid more money and required fewer hours," she concedes, "but I've been really happy with my career and what I've done."

As a leader, Bonnie's management style is heavily oriented around goals, targets, and benchmarks. Utilizing these tools to both measure and motivate, her job is to set strategies and then allow her team to implement them. "I'm considerably structured but still laissez-faire," she remarks of her commitment to allowing her team to operate without her interference. "I'm not going to get in their business, but if they get in a ditch, I want to know about it." Her leadership strengths are further highlighted through her ability to recognize the fortes of a given individual and then match those strengths to their ideal position within the overall enterprise. She then cements compatible and efficient employee webs through team building exercises that maximize interaction and understanding amongst the various levels of staff.

Inherent in the intricacies of this leadership style is a commitment to mentor her staff, ensuring that her employees have the tools they need to advance in their career. This dedication stems in part from the role of a mentor in her own life, which was filled by the CFO she worked for at her first hospital job in Georgia. Identifying an unusual proficiency in her, he allowed her to be a controller even before she received her degree and was later the person who convinced her to get her Masters. As a mentor, he was able to identify and promote the inherent sense of confidence she had always seen in herself, which she identifies as a product of the very unique political climate in which she was raised. "Growing up in the sixties along with the experiences of Martin Luther King and John F. Kennedy imparted the belief that anybody could do anything they put their mind to," she recalls. "Even though a lot of that period was tragic, there was also a headiness to it. It showed that you didn't have to be a white male born into millions of dollars in order to be successful."

Such an observation hits on one of the most fascinating aspects of Bonnie's perspective—her ability to place her development and career within its historical context. Life does not exist in a vacuum, and she readily relates her values and philosophies to specific national events and trends. In doing this, others who lived through the same events can easily plug into her experiences, and those who were born later can at least learn from her example. Thus, to future entrepreneurs entering the workforce, Bonnie stresses the importance of this interplay between context and passion in choosing one's ideal path. "Look around you at the messages being conveyed through your particular place in history," she urges. "Pay attention to what moves you and carry that with you throughout your life." By identifying this passion and compounding it with the power of education, one's capacity for greatness is truly limitless.

Fouad Qreitem

When Business is Personal

"You guys make the best food," remarked the man, as he laid down the bills to pay for his pizza. "Not to mention that your customer service is amazing. How come I've never heard of you?"

"We're new," remarked Fouad Qreitem, President and CEO of Paisano's Pizza Restaurant.

It was 1999, less than a year after Paisano's had first opened its doors. The man thanked Fouad and left the store to its typical hustle and bustle, but the small restaurant's luck was about to change forever. Three weeks later, an article was published in the Washington Post recounting the exceptional quality and service of a certain local hidden-gem pizza joint, written by the very same man who had so generously complemented its young owner. "Almost immediately after the write-up hit newsstands, our business doubled," Fouad remembers.

At twenty-four years of age, Fouad founded Paisano's in 1998 along with his sister, Cathy, when the pair opened their first store in Fair Lakes. Cathy stayed with the company for the first four to five years of the endeavor, a time of backbreaking work and high tension, as they didn't receive a paycheck for the entirety of their first year in business. "Until you've worked for free, you don't know what work is," he remarks now, still incredulous at the thought of his twelve-hour workdays and sometimes seven-day workweeks. When he married in 1999, he took only four days off for his honeymoon. "I definitely paid my dues," he says. "Still, I enjoyed it because I knew it was all me. I knew that if I failed, at least it would be because of me and not because of somebody else."

Thankfully, Fouad led Paisano's down a far different road and never had to confront such failure. In fact, his flagship store has maintained a minimum growth rate of twenty percent for each of the thirteen years since it opened. The restaurant incurred so much positive attention that he opened another one in 2001, cementing his original success into systematic operations that he could then replicate in new environments. After the subsequent opening five additional stores, he then decided to transition Paisano's into a franchise in June of 2009. The groundwork for the initiative took a year and a half to complete, and now with the operation in its fledgling stages, six franchises have been sold so far. With two already open and two more scheduled to open in the fourth quarter of 2010, still others are slated to follow soon after. Fouad ultimately hopes to own twenty corporate stores as is particularly excited about his upcoming Tyson's Corner location, scheduled to open later this year.

Surprisingly, Paisano's is exactly the opposite of what franchisees would have been looking for seven to ten years ago. With a menu that is varied and complex, previous models would have deemed it to expansive to replicate, with franchise restaurants typically sticking with menus of several simple items. Now, however, the trend is toward diversity, and

Paisano's is poised far ahead of the curve. "The secret to our success has been our continued ability to provide quality menu choices with items to satisfy a wide range of tastes and using only the best ingredients," Fouad explains. "There is really something for everyone."

While many people struggle with finding their passion and vocation in life, Fouad knew from an early age that his professional path lay in the restaurant business. In fact, when his sixth grade class penned pictures of their futures for a time capsule that would be opened many years down the line, Fouad's portrait mirrored today's reality to a tee. This sense of certainty stemmed in part from the thorough immersion he had in the industry from a very early age, as his father and uncles were restaurant owners themselves. The men owned The Black Orchid, a French continental cuisine restaurant that was recognized as one of the best in the area. They also opened a small dine-in and delivery pizza place down the street. He hired top chefs for each of his establishments, which did wonders for The Black Orchid but made little economical sense for the pizzeria—a fact that Fouad would note and put into practice later in his own business.

Fouad was five years old when his father first opened the pizza establishment, and he was always envious of his cousins who got to have the "fun" job delivering pizzas while he was stuck in the fine dining restaurant. From the time he was very young, he can remember his parents' unwavering commitment to the restaurants and recalls instances in which they would stop by the establishments on their days off with the children and spend hours enmeshed in the business. Beginning at age ten, Fouad would work as well, hanging coats and manning the coffee station. "I didn't have much of a childhood," he remarks now. He later graduated on to dishwashing and eventually served as *maitre d'*. "As a teenager I would get out of school at 2:30, arrive at the restaurant by 4:30, and then wouldn't get home till around 12:00 A.M," he reports.

While many people assume that his present-day success stems from the work-oriented environment he knew in his youth, Fouad is not so sure. He did, however, have the opportunity to observe his father's unparalleled customer service skills, which he acknowledges as being paramount in shaping his leadership style. "As soon as someone would become somewhat regular, my father would give them the royal treatment. Even if there was a line out the door, he would spot you and drag you in to a table you didn't even call to reserve," Fouad laughs. "You can't find his level of attentiveness anywhere today." Fouad has modeled his own customer service as such, striving to always go above and beyond to turn every customer interaction into an exceptional experience. Each customer call is recorded in a log sheet, and managers follow up with any issue in which someone may not be 100 percent satisfied with their experience. These kinds of safety nets are designed such that no customer service issue slips through the cracks, and it has paid back in spades over the years.

Another key to the success of Paisano's has been a business model in which administrative and overhead matters are largely performed by one office, thereby allowing store managers to focus solely on customer service, product quality, payroll, and scheduling. "I then supplement this by meeting with the managers weekly to have an open table group discussion," says Fouad. "We go through an agenda and discuss our ideas, focusing on what works and what doesn't work."

When he isn't engaged in these meetings, he is engaged in other meetings. In fact, Fouad spends three days a week just meeting with vendors and brokers, working hard to keep each restaurant up to his standards while adding new establishments to the map. Despite this flurry of activity, however, he prioritizes time at home with his family as well. "My two girls are my greatest successes," he says of his daughters, age nine and five. "As children, we became self-sufficient at a young age because both our parents worked such long hours at the restaurants to provide for us." Thus, balancing family with work is of the utmost importance to him now. He achieves this balance largely through the dedication and strength of his wife, who serves as an unparalleled support system in his life.

The key to attaining a success in which this work-life balance is possible, according to Fouad, is to maintain a rock-solid work ethic in which one sets goals and then meets or exceeds them every time. "People used to tell me I wasn't going to make it, but this would just fuel my conviction more," he reflects. He also maintains a "no excuse" policy to guide the journey of accomplishing these goals and would advise any young entrepreneur today to do the same. "You can always come up with a reason for why business is bad, no matter what the season," he says. "Instead, commit yourself to the expectation that business should be good year-round." Maintaining this mindset places one in a very unique category; one that isn't common in today's marketplace.

This commitment to setting and surpassing goals spills over into the philanthropic activities of the company as well. Fouad has been particularly committed to the Police Unity Tour, a bike ride honoring law enforcement officers who lost their lives in the line of duty and aiming to raise money for the National Law Enforcement Officers Memorial and Museum. Paisano's aims to raise $100,000 for the cause in 2011. The restaurant also supports Rachel D'Andrea, a little girl from the local community with a rare and deadly form of cancer, by donating two dollars from every large pizza sold on Monday nights to her fund. The funds assist with the mounting debt her parents are incurring for medical expenses, allowing them to focus more time on Rachel. Additionally, after Thanksgiving, all Paisano's locations set up a drop-off donation box collecting canned goods for people in need. "Helping people in Fairfax county means a lot to me," Fouad explains.

This mindset is perfectly in keeping with the overarching tenet behind the Paisano's philosophy, which is firmly committed to the strong personal relationships characterizing everything they do. "I always encourage our managers to develop relationships with our clients," says Fouad. The ideology at work behind the company is that every person must be considered a valued customer from their very first order. Having a genuine passion and sincere concern about each individual's experience is something Fouad has never regretted, especially when he ventures into his original store in Fair Lakes and spends time just chatting with old friends and customers. It makes sense, then, that despite his tremendous plans for continued franchising, he hopes to keep his stores local. Contracted to have fifty locations throughout the DC metro area in the next five years, he still hopes to be able to get in his car and visit different stores, continuing to develop the kind of relationships that have gotten him to where he is today. "I love what I do," he emphasizes. "It's not just about money, it's personal."

Roger Sandau

The Dimensions of a Dream

Tap tap tap, went the ruler on the shining wood of the piano. Roger Sandau peered up begrudgingly at his instructor, a stern woman whose face and demeanor wore a permanent scowl. He tried to keep his playing in time with her metronomic tapping, but truth be told, he found little gratification in the task. The young boy loved to watch his father play, taken with the immediacy of the creation of music before his very eyes, but did not enjoy the task himself. It wasn't until the age of thirteen, when he sat down to play at a friend's house and was immediately surrounded by dreamy-eyed girls, that his perception of the art changed. "I realized the ability to play music has an attraction to people and creates an emotion in the audience that is unlike anything else," he remembers. "I suddenly saw it possessed the unique ability to transcend cultural, linguistic, geographic, and social boundaries." Now the CEO of Doodson Insurance Brokerage LLC, Roger has created the opportunity to build his career around his passion—though not exactly in the way he originally planned.

After igniting his flair for playing and composing as a young teen, he started his freshman year of college with a roommate who, much to his delight, had been a traveling musician. "He was the first person I had ever met who had actually made a record," Roger marvels. The relationship allowed him to bridge the mental gap between goal and reality, and suddenly a light went off. After meeting people who had successfully navigated the music business and seeing that it was possible to put out a record, Roger wanted to be a musician.

With this vision clear in his mind, he graduated college and left town for San Francisco, where he joined a band and played every opportunity that came his way in the hopes of being discovered. Despite this total immersion, however, he eventually found that success was not happening as fast as he had hoped or expected. Instead of abandoning his dream, Roger instead set about redrafting his mental blueprints. Noting that the music business was largely run by lawyers, he decided to go to law school while continuing to play. The strategy bought him three more years to pursue his dream while also developing a career that would be a good entry point into the business if his Plan A didn't pan out. When he hadn't realized a record deal by the time of his graduation and completion of the bar exam, his brief career as a professional musician ended and his new career as an entertainment lawyer commenced.

Following a decade of representing musicians, concert promoters, record companies and music publishers, Roger transitioned from his legal practice to the insurance industry, upon discovering the existence of specialized insurance products designed for the music and touring industries. In 1995, by a purely fortuitous stroke of curiosity and luck, he answered a classified ad in an entertainment magazine to work with a popular musical group known as The Three Tenors. Luciano Pavarotti, among the most commercially successful tenors to date, was one of its members. The musicians invested considerable funds each time they performed a show, always aiming to present a stadium-quality performance but also wary of the high cost and impossibility of rescheduling a show should something go wrong. Thus, Roger sought to ensure that they had proper coverage for such financial risks. "It was truly a turning point for me," he remembers. "If I hadn't gotten involved with them, I wouldn't have developed an appreciation for this unique aspect of the insurance industry."

Several years later, as The Three Tenors approached retirement, Roger found himself looking for an interim career move amidst the boom of the dot-come era. Struck by the idea of using the internet to sell wedding insurance, he set about researching. The concept was not yet widely available in the US, but it had a proven track record as an insurance product in the UK, so he signed deals with two major wedding portals and launched the company that would broaden his experience of the insurance industry. WedSafe became one of the first companies to sell insurance products online, developing all the technology to deliver their services through electronic means.

Though solid in its initial conceptualization, the fall of the dot-come era left WedSafe unsellable in 2001. "With the devastation and uncertainty caused by the events of 9/11, the insurance industry was a mess, and we wrestled with keeping an insurance carrier to support the program," Roger recalls. Political and social context improved, however, and the company was finally acquired in 2005 by a Fortune 250 company called Aon. Through this experience, he was appointed CEO of Robertson Taylor Insurance Brokers, becoming deeply enmeshed in the music and touring insurance business. After running Robertson Taylor for over four years, he departed to work as the Chief Operating Officer of an insurance captive for a short time and then decided to set up his own insurance brokerage firm. Thus, Crossfields Insurance Brokerage, LLC, was born.

Rather than building a large specialty infrastructure, his business model focused on constructing a fabric of strategic partnerships with outside firms. Strong client relationships were the cornerstones of the enterprise, and this model enabled him to service particular client needs without having to build specific infrastructure for each type of coverage need. Such needs generally included niche insurance products applicable to the entertainment, sports, and leisure industries, such as non-appearance and event cancellation coverage, high limit disability coverage, contract bonus coverage, and an assortment of commercial insurance products as well.

After building Crossfields into a prominent player in the US music and entertainment insurance industry, Roger was approached by Arthur Doodson Brokers Ltd, a leading independent insurance brokerage firm in the United Kingdom founded in 1964 and specializing in entertainment. The firm had created an umbrella organization known as Doodson Broking Group to represent the various companies in which they held majority or full ownership. Through a number of acquisitions, the organization had come to house three different UK firms, which currently sit somewhere along the continuum of absorption into Arthur Doodson Brokers. The company was looking to expand into the US and was familiar with Roger's background with Robertson Taylor, their most significant competitor in the UK. They contacted Roger with the hopes of integrating Crossfields into their business, with Roger himself spearheading the growth of Arthur Doodson on the US. Thus, in early 2010, the company merged with Crossfields to create an international live music and entertainment insurance enterprise, and Crossfields changed its corporate name to Doodson Insurance Brokerage, LLC, to reflect its status as a fully-owned subsidiary of the corporation.

The opportunity to merge Crossfields with Doodson Broking Group was the perfect opportunity arriving at the perfect time for Roger, granting him the capacity to, for example, work with the largest concert promoter in the world. It also provided him with immediate liquidity of his equity in the company, which posed a tremendous advantage. Furthermore, it afforded the possibility of leaving a larger global footprint, serving international clients he might have otherwise lacked the capacity to handle. Crossfields had reached a point at which it needed a larger service platform to work with more weighty and expansive clients, while Doodson had reached a point at which it had successfully transitioned from an entrepreneurial single-owner business to a multi-owner business while still maintaining its status as a closely held corporation. Equipped with a young and forward-facing management team, Roger felt as though both businesses were poised to truly pursue their growth through the synergistic partnership.

If one were to go back in time and ask a younger Roger where he projected his professional path to lead, the chances of a reference to the entertainment insurance industry are slim to none. Yet it is precisely this unanticipated plot twist that renders his story so compelling. While so many young people give up on their dreams when reality confounds their options, Roger saw that reality, though harsh, was not uncompromising. Though his path did not go exactly as originally planned, he has built a career that continues to emulate the principles of music that first impassioned him. "I grew up in a house where my mother played the piano, so music has always been a very tangible experience for me," Roger stresses. He observed how it brought people together and allowed them to participate, and he feels a similar sense of unity, engagement, and immediacy when he promotes and witnesses live performances today. "It's the same shared experience and sense of community that draws people to music and keeps the industry going now," he remarks.

Roger's secret to success seems to be three-fold. First, he advises an ongoing investment in technical knowledge about your chosen field. This is then supplemented by a true passion for the information and work at hand. With these two tools, individuals will be prepared to succeed in whatever opportunity may arise. "As you go through your career, you'll be presented with various opportunities through people that you meet. Relationships lead to opportunities and you can decide to either pursue a given opportunity, or determine that it's not right for you at the time," Roger advises.

Beyond this advice, Roger's background exhibits a resolve, resilience, and optimistic realism that seem to be built into the very fabric of his character. This is particularly fascinating in light of the fact that his maternal grandparents were Holocaust survivors and had a tremendously challenging path through life, having struggled through labor camps in Munich and then a displaced persons camp in Germany. After witnessing one stillbirth and then one child who died from the mass inoculations required before immigrating to the US, they crossed the Atlantic to a foreign land without speaking any English. "By their very nature, they were survival people," Roger proclaims. "They were people who had faced some of the greatest obstacles in life and had persevered with diligence, hard work, prudence, and tenacity. I see myself as continuing along this trajectory, and whenever I'm facing obstacles, I think of what my grandparents had to go through and see that the challenges I'm facing aren't that formidable."

This perspective is a valuable tool whenever one pushes toward some form of success, whether releasing a new piece of music into the world or seeking to transform a company through innovative theory and action. "Our greatest challenges and, conversely, our greatest successes will always be taking an idea and seeing how far it can go," says Roger. "We create something and then put it out there for people to judge. The ability to do this is what advances the world forward, and actually seeing the result of your idea can be the greatest reward imaginable." Whether your dream is artistic, entrepreneurial, business-oriented, or life-oriented, these universal principles help ensure that, despite obstacles, we allow our ideas and ourselves to achieve their full potential.

Keith Scott

The Spirit of Business

For most Americans, the concept of family dinner invokes warm feelings of leisurely chatting and lighthearted banter around the table as the day unwinds. Keith Scott's family, however, did no such thing. With Keith being the only child of a father who spent 40 years working for the National Security Agency, dinner was instead reserved as the perfect time to hone the family's debate skills.

"I remember sitting around the kitchen table at dinners as a kid, always posing fair, structured arguments about current events or political issues," he recalls. "I grew up believing that you should always make sure that you can verbally express your message and that you should be able to counter any point in an argument." Now the President and CEO of the Baltimore County Chamber of Commerce, Keith advocates in the interest of business through employing the very same skills of quick wit, articulation, and tenacity that kept him on his toes at the dinner table all those years ago.

The Chamber invests a large portion of its time and resources into one of its main objectives, which is fulfilling its role as a legislative watchdog and combating the threat of over-regulation to ensure that businesses have the flexibility they need to promote innovation. "Our number one issue is looking at legislation and making sure it doesn't unfairly impose burdensome regulations on businesses. The more burdensome a regulation is, the more it chokes the human entrepreneurial spirit," he emphasizes. "We believe as a Chamber that the free market system promotes the ability of people to think in new and creative ways. It's the spirit of business—the economic engine of this country." Keith and his team continually observe and participate in this spirit by maintaining a constant presence at community events. "We want the Chamber to be forward thinking, present, and known that it is a resource that understands the pulse of what's going on in the community," he emphasizes.

The Chamber's other objective, which fills the rest of its time and resources, is to serve as a networking service for business leaders, lending a human element to the process that is often lacking in today's networking landscape. "You can have a million contacts on Facebook or LinkedIn, but you can't truly build relationships until you meet someone face to face, look them in the eye and realize that you have chemistry and trust," Keith observes.

Because 23 percent of its membership base is located in the city of Baltimore, the Chamber works hand in hand with the Baltimore City Chamber of Commerce to accomplish these goals. With member businesses and approximately 210,000 employees, the Chamber is currently seeing its fastest membership growth in the city. "In seeking to expand our membership, we've been very proactive in finding new types of industries and in reaching out to new and upstart businesses," Keith reflects.

While the Chamber used to serve a relatively homogenized sampling of lawyers, accountants, and bankers, it has since expanded its vision substantially to include other industries such as the arts, nonprofits and upstart businesses. This kind of diversity benefits all members by keeping the Chamber strong even as certain sectors face times of hardship. Its vision doesn't stop there, embracing green and alternative energy businesses while also focusing its efforts on drawing smaller businesses with strong growth potential. Thanks to these innovative and forward thinking efforts, the Chamber has sustained itself quite well during the current economic downfall as compared to other chambers and businesses. "Our ability to maintain revenues stems from careful cost-cutting measures combined with creative collaboration, analyzing our concentrations and figuring out how to tap very nontraditional sources of income," Keith explains.

These strategies have been further supplemented by the "givers gain" philosophy that Keith so strongly advocates. Rejecting the silo mentality that many businesses and chambers maintain, he and his team have been working with other groups like the Hispanic Chamber of Commerce and the African American Chamber of Commerce. Such partnerships are mutually beneficial and allow all parties to grow and, in turn, more businesses to benefit. "So many firms don't realize that, if they're not part of an organized body, the government is more likely to target them for regulations. The more people and organizations they have to fight for them, the better off they'll be," Keith remarks. "You don't want to be the lone weak deer in the forest."

Keith acquired his first job when he was 16 years old at a Catholic retreat center, cooking and serving meals to nuns who had taken a vow of silence. His favorite work experience as a young man was working as an overnight camp counselor challenging children to expand their character, and this appreciation likely stemmed in large part from his own intense response to an Outward Bound trip he had participated in during high school. "It was one of the worst experiences I have ever had, but among the best in terms of self development and self esteem building," he reflects, as he recounts falling out of a canoe and almost getting hypothermia or walking twelve miles just to run out of water and have to eat freeze dried food. "It really taught me the value of what I had and what I could accomplish."

Keith's college career was checkered between four different universities, one of which lent an element of international experience through its location in Germany, and he was afforded tremendous opportunity to hone his debate skills through attempting to transfer his credits so frequently. After ultimately graduating from the University of Maryland at Baltimore County with a degree in Political Science, he moved to West Virginia where he ran for a school board on a whim and won the election over eleven other candidates. He later spent some time working for a global staffing company called Adecco, which gave him intimate behind-the-scenes understanding of a vast array of companies and the culture of business behind each.

Keith also spent over seven years working with Goodwill Industries in Frederick and Hagerstown, MD, traveling around the country as he participated in their executive leadership program. "This experience gave me an excellent understanding on how to start and maintain a business, building out the staff and dealing with issues like quotas, industrial needs, and production," he reports. The wealth of knowledge gained through these positions set a perfect stage for what was to follow.

Keith's journey with the Baltimore County Chamber began in 2007 when he accepted a position as Director of Government Relations, which was essentially a grooming position for his ascension to the position of CEO. After spending a year observing and partnering with the previous CEO to learn the needs of the Chamber and its members, he had established a level of trust with the Board of Directors and assumed the position of CEO in 2008. "My main objective during that time was to bridge the gap between the old way and the new way in terms of how the Chamber would be run," Keith remembers. "Because our networking groups had expanded, we needed to prove our niche, as well as the vital importance of incorporating other niches."

Because he was considerably younger than many of the Chamber and Board members, Keith had much to prove in his early months, demonstrating that the organization could handle a different leadership style and ideas while still turning a profit and maintaining its growth. "That's the gentle balance that a leader has to have coming in," he explains. "You have to make sure you don't alienate the constituency that's built the enterprise over the years but still implement new, outside-the-box ideas."

Not only was the Board looking for someone who could instill a sense of balance and trust, but also someone with the tenacity of a true go-getter. "I won't stop until I get what we need for the Chamber, whether it's legislative lobbying or funding," Keith confirms. "If we had a bill that needed to pass, I wouldn't stop working the phones or visiting the hallways or meeting with people until we got it approved." This is accomplished in large part through the unusually compelling, persuasive, and motivating qualities in his character—the kind that truly inspire others to act. "The biggest part of leadership as a CEO is inspiring people to greatness and to realize that they can do it. The word *can't* should never be uttered—it's really just a deferred yes," says Keith. By infusing the spirit of business with this element of steadfast resolve, Keith repeatedly demonstrates that the Chamber can accomplish anything so long as it's willing to invest the energy and roll up its sleeves to make it happen.

In addition to the tenacity emanating from all aspects of his character, Keith stresses the importance of exercising creative problem solving when it comes to leadership. "You have to constantly pivot," he explains. "Some days you'll lay seeds that will germinate over a long period of time, while other days you'll be dealing with issues that require immediate attention. You have to be able to utilize different avenues, rules, and techniques to get you and your organization to where it needs to be."

Though his can-do attitude stems primarily from his father's influence, Keith also traces it to the impact of various prominent historical players. With an ancestry that hails from Scotland, he notes that the fierce determination and tenacity defining his work ethic mirror that which fueled the Scottish resistance to English rule centuries ago. Similarly, his progressive and innovative mindset borrowed largely from the examples set by the Founding Fathers of the U.S., who refused to accept the status quo and instead tested the limits of what life readily offered them. "The dreamers, the people who develop businesses, the people who helped build this country—all were tremendous risk takers who weren't afraid to test the status quo," says Keith.

The Founding Fathers, as well, were pioneers and leaders in all that they did, developing a wide range of skills that ultimately made them more well-rounded, influential individuals, and Keith is quick to follow in their lead. In his spare time, he participates in art to promote self-expression and singing to strengthen his public speaking skills in the sense that both activities emphasize a point and create an emotion between the sender and receiver through tonal value. Now a public speaking instructor at the college level, he also engages in improvisation acting, which stretches the limits of his comfort zone through public performance and utilizes the physical body as an important component of nonverbal communication. "I like to do things that get your mind moving quickly because you have to be that way in the business world," he stresses. "I am a tremendous believer in the renaissance theory of self development because a multifaceted set of talents act as building blocks to make you a better person and leader."

Keith's greatest piece of advice to young entrepreneurs entering the business world today, then, is the importance of releasing one's self-consciousness, even in the midst of judgment from others. "Ego can be a good motivator, but it can also be a huge threat to success by holding us back," Keith points out. "If you can deflate your ego and always be the first to volunteer, the first to test the waters, or the first to risk embarrassment, you will dive into the dynamic and vibrant world in which we live." In this manner, one can attain the can-do, will-do, free thinking attitude that Keith has passed on to his own children and that eliminates the barriers between what is doubted and what can be accomplished.

George Spears

The What-If Strategy

Most people go through life looking for answers. George Spears, on the other hand, goes through life looking for questions. His Myers-Briggs results proclaim him a researcher at heart, and anyone with the opportunity to observe his lived manner and style would confirm the edict. Now the President of Equipment Solutions Inc., a manufacturer representative company serving the DC metro area and specializing in the restaurant industry, George's unique deliberation in goal achievement centers on the development of an intricate sequence of what-if questions and helpful hypotheticals.

In much the same way Michelangelo stared at his block of marble for weeks on end before creating the Statue of David, George develops sophisticated mental constructs and considerations before setting to work in stone. The mental acrobatics of the strategy may be protracted and exhausting, but in the end, masterpieces are born.

Taking a peak under the hood, Equipment Solutions is, at first glance, a sales and marketing firm. Digging a little deeper, however, one finds elements of a manufacturer's rep firm and a brokerage model at play in the mix as well. The company's business model aims to resell products from high-quality manufacturers through a virtual sales force of five hundred representatives overseen by five managers working from 170 independent dealer firms dispersed throughout the region. Equipped with this small army, the company effectively coordinates the efforts of dealers selling products, consultants and architects designing buildings, and larger chains like the Marriott Corporation, orchestrating both successful relationships and profitable transactions.

What truly makes Equipment Solutions stand out against the backdrop of its competition is the organization lent through its infrastructure, which has been built up at a steady pace over the past three years. Their office is now outfitted to swiftly intake and output exceptionally high volumes, operating as leanly as possible. George has helped to define and promote these outstanding qualities through his focused attention on organizational development through sound infrastructure and team building.

When George graduated from Washington & Lee University in 1982 with a liberal arts degree, he would never have guessed how his future would unfold. "I was a typical kid with little direction. Nothing in college had particularly clicked for me," he admits. Without a specific path in mind, he accepted a position as a project manager for a firm that built commercial kitchens. His five years at the company lent tremendous experience, allowing him to work on a number of large projects in New York and DC. Coincidentally, he came to learn about the various manufacturers he now works with through these projects, and it was only a matter of time before they approached him to see if he had any interest in transitioning over to the sales side of the industry. After earning his MBA from Marymount University in 1990, that's precisely what he did.

George's first experience in the manufacturer's rep business came in the form of an independent contractor position, which quickly evolved into a partnership opportunity. During the next eleven years, he served as a Principal for both Mid-Atlantic Marketing Agents, Inc. and Target Distributing, Inc. These firms served as manufacturers' representatives, a regional distributor, and coordinated installation experts nationwide. These early experiences provided an abundance of growth opportunities, and George gained nuanced expertise until one of his business partners decided to move on in 2001.

The equity of the companies was liquidated, and George seized the day by co-founding Equipment Solutions. With the promise and opportunity of a clean slate, he and his partner envisioned an enterprise that operated as a pure outsourcing sales and marketing company free of the ancillary activity that had weighed down their past businesses. Additionally, they started a healthcare rep firm known as Facilities Services, Inc. This company translated the skills and services provided by their other endeavors into a different industry, which quickly evolved into a Restaurant Equipment Dealership and was spun off shortly thereafter to avoid any potential conflict of interest.

With a finance and business background, George's emergence on and subsequent mastery of the restaurant business presents an astounding contrast. Though he had always enjoyed the practice and art involved in both creating and consuming a culinary project, it was the general business framework rather than the specific industry that first captivated him. "An opportunity was presented to me that just happened to be in the restaurant industry, and I was intrigued by the model and by the concept of volume," he remembers. "I'm a very visual guy and a very transactional guy. I was fascinated with the process of putting an organization together and the way a volume of sales is channeled through it."

Though well equipped with solid industry knowledge, starting a company does not come without sacrifice. "You bet on the roll," says

George. "When I first got into [the business], I didn't have two nickels to scrape together." His start-up strategy was relatively straightforward: betting that if they worked hard, their sales pipeline would outpace their expense pipeline at some point and they would break even. The bet paid off.

For Equipment Solutions, break-even came ten months after first opening its doors. Shortly afterward, George continued to advance the business model by merging the enterprise with a company that specialized in furnishing and decorative aspects to create a highly diversified rep firm. The culmination of these moves results in a firm that today serves to bring buyers and sellers together and to act as a key player in the transactional process that ensues.

In many ways, the business George has chiseled out resembles a living body with its various pivotal facets. The strong infrastructure provides a skeletal framework, while the heart and lifeblood of the company is customer service and relationship building. The entity is then completed by the management of information, keeping internal records of all the facts and figures that affect the players they work with and monitoring them closely.

Analyzing the numbers weekly, monthly, quarterly, yearly, and by year-to-date, George delineates patterns indicating whether they're keeping stride or not. In essence, he tracks the inhale, exhale, and heartbeat of the enterprise.

Since its inception in 2002, Equipment Solutions has evolved from six manufacturers to twenty-four. Sales have undergone a similar amplification, leaping from four to five million dollars in its first year of business to thirteen million today. This upward trajectory stems in large part from its consistent focus on diversifying its product portfolio and then providing its salespeople with responsive and comprehensive support. Whether it's organizational, design, technical, or sales assistance, the ultimate aim is to provide a complete toolset for smooth transactions from inception to completion.

Despite such incontrovertible success thus far, George's story is far from finished. "We all have our own personal goals," he acknowledges. "Mine is to do something larger. I've had a taste of what it's like to develop a business, and I want to take this to the next level." With its infrastructure intact and streamlined, Equipment Solutions is poised to plug other components into its process quite seamlessly. As such, the company's horizon is far from certain.

As George would quickly remind us, however, success does not occur in isolation. Considering his propensity for gathering and synthesizing new information, it comes as no surprise that he is particularly drawn to leadership groups. Having participated in such organizations for the past two years, he has had the invaluable opportunity to survey and analyze a vast array of people he would otherwise never have met. "Being exposed to so many different ideas has been such an eye-opener," he stresses. "I've had a chance to see how different business models and best practices work within big and small companies, and all from a leadership perspective."

By supplementing these experiences with his own reading and research, he considers the current epoch of his life to be somewhat of an apprenticeship—a time for him to observe and absorb to see how it all works.

Perhaps the most profound impact this research inclination has had on Equipment Solutions is its propensity for genuine reflection. With a leadership philosophy that revolves around open-mindedness, George holds it paramount to examine all possible courses of action in the face of a particular end-gain. "My style is to make sure that all questions are asked before a decision is made," he confirms.

This is attained through posing a vast array of "why" and "what if" queries aimed at uncovering and weighing the theoretical underpinnings of each and every decision. Not only does this process lead to an educated and sound outcome, but it also inspires strong commiseration and support from others involved. "It is a path toward credibility,"

George explains. "Everybody ends up sharing the same goal, and if someone falls off, it's easier to collectively pull them back on board."

The what-if game is applicable not only in day-to-day decision making, but also in the grand scheme of a life's trajectory. Despite his characteristic laid-back demeanor, he demands a full-blown inquisition in this regard, particularly when young entrepreneurs find themselves entering the workforce. "First, ask yourself very pointedly what your end-gain is. Then ask why? Why, why, why?" he emphasizes. "Next, ask yourself if you have the aspiration to own your own business or if the corporate world is more up your alley. Do some serious soul-searching; some serious why-asking."

Thus, the constant theme radiating through George's strategy and influence is to start with the end in mind in order to conceptualize of your immediate options. In other words, don't set a chisel to your marble before you have a complete and radiating image of David in your mind's eye. After all, it is precisely this ability to start with an envisioned end-gain and work backward that truly allows us to move forward in our professions and our lives.

Richard Toren

The Art (and Heart) of Invention

When he's out on the green after a long week at work, Richard Toren isn't exactly switching gears. Though there is arguably a clear distinction between his role as President and Chairman of the Board for CodeRyte and his role as a golfer amidst the tranquility of the course, the philosophies at work—or play—are much the same. Both environments are shaped by competition, and both are reliant upon character traits like patience, focus, and a strong drive in order to sink the ball in the hole. And, while golf may differ from business in its margin for ethical error, one must ultimately answer to either the spectators or to oneself. If you employ golf ethics within your business practice, refusing to cut corners and exhibiting honesty and integrity in your endeavors, you're on the track for birdie over bogie, as Rick's ideology dictates.

This system of unassuming tenacity and firm ethics has been a part of Rick's life since early childhood. Even at such a young age, he held the concept of independence to be paramount and worked to raise money mowing lawns and shoveling snow in elementary school. His entrepreneurial flare shone first as he orchestrated a small lawn mowing business to maximize profitability, and again later in college when he started a small franchise that installed and managed pinball machines in the frat houses of Penn State. This business, his first sale, went for $10,000 when he graduated.

Rick's road to CodeRyte, his current enterprise, has been an ever-escalating series of luck and proactivity. He found himself fresh out of college in the midst of the Vietnam War, barred from service due to a basketball injury to the knee. It was an era saturated with an inimitable air of sorrow and opportunity. With a father in dentistry and an older brother in cardiology, he had always been drawn to the healthcare field but possessed an innovative, solutions-oriented, persuasive edge that seemed to suggest there was something more in the cards for him than his premed pursuit. Upon graduating, he went to work for American Hospice Supply in Chicago selling IV solutions, which equipped him with sales skills as well as a nuanced understanding of hospital culture. It was there that he first exercised what many would term his greatest gift—the ability to turn pain into progress. Observing the ineffective protocol for administering nutrition intravenously to sick children, he proposed a reformed procedure that resulted in the organization's most profitable product. Then, confronted with an opportunity to move to the DC area to work for a small start-up company developing injection technology, Rick promptly dropped out of graduate school and joined forces with Survival Technology Inc.

The very definition of a serial entrepreneur, Rick has started five separate companies since those early days of his career. Through an array of ups and downs saturated with risk and reward, the majority of these ventures have proven wildly successful. CodeRyte, established by Rick in 1999 after a brief year-long stint as a retiree, was among them, and was actually launched simultaneously with two other businesses. Realizing the breadth of his obligation, he hired Andy Kapit to serve as CEO of CodeRyte throughout its early years as he focused on developing EMedics, which eventually merged with Active Health and was sold to AETNA in 2004 for $400 million. Since then, he has focused the majority of his time at CodeRyte.

Though considerably sophisticated in its details, the concept behind the company is exceedingly straightforward in its logic. It serves to fill the gap between physician services and physician billing. Billing, in the medical field, is reported through a network of codes, and because doctors prioritize their medical obligations, they often misreport these codes when detailing their services to insurance companies. The technology employed here is not only unique, but also translatable across fields. Codes might be used, for example, to identify and correct medical mistakes or malpractice. At this point, the possibilities are endless.

In breaking Rick's evident success into its component parts, a primary element can be identified in the words of his favorite mantra: good ideas are a dime a dozen—it's the execution that makes all the difference. Believing wholeheartedly in the truth to this proverb, Rick spends several hours each week mentoring for the Network for Teaching Entrepreneurship (NFTE), an organization committed to helping youth in low-income communities unleash their creativity and entrepreneurial potential. As he would advise any young person at the brink of entering the workforce, he teaches his mentees about the importance of follow through with your intentions—an outcome best achieved through conceptualization proceeded by implementation. When struck with an idea, he advises, try to project what life would look and feel like once it is executed. Determine whether the idea will add value, meaning, and happiness to your life once it has reached fruition. Develop strategies in advance and engage others in debate. And most importantly, develop poise and a strong comfort level with public speaking so that your idea can truly be heard.

Looking at his group of high school mentees as a microcosm reflection of his workplace, one can imagine that the relationship he holds with staff is one of mutual respect and development. Considered an ennabler by those who know him, he strives to lead by example in terms of energy and dedication. One finds it harder, however, to categorize him as primarily detail-oriented or more of a big-picture leader. While his innovative background accentuates his fine-slicer tendencies, his credible forward-thinking and his all-encompassing grasp of the processes at work speak to his broad perspective. It is this unique pairing of traits that he credits for his own success, and it is likewise this unique pairing of traits that he hopes to see in the younger workforce.

In addition to the strong emphasis on follow-through, the other trait most boldly pronounced through Rick's success is the very personal and heartfelt spin he has invested in so many of his innovations. When the general population is faced with obstacles in life, we are apt to search for the best possible solution given the available options. What happens, however, if the available options aren't good enough? Well, if you're Richard Toren, you invent new ones. This has always been his philosophy, and his life's work has thus become the embodiment of that first instance where the inadequacy of intravenous nutrition spurred him to develop an entirely new product for malnourished children.

Nowhere is this ability to transform pain into progress better exemplified than in the story of his youngest daughter, who suffers from severe allergic reactions to bee stings. In the 1970s, there was no product specifically designed to be self-administered if a hypersensitive individual was stung, so Rick came up with the EpiPen and worked closely with engineers to develop the device. This combination of innovation and heart closely parallels an earlier incident in which one of his newborn children was placed in intensive care and monitored with an EKG. Rick observed that the electrodes used in this process would tear the fragile skin of the newborns, so he used a new carbon-impregnated plastic material to create a glue-free electrode that was gentle and pain-free.

Whether he is solving the acute pain of a loved one or the more generalized pain of medical coding inefficiencies, the ability to target and solve such ailments speaks to a vein of empathy and humanity that is rarely so manifest. We are all taught lessons of humility and heart at different times in our lives and by different teachers; for Rick, the teacher was his own son. When the boy finally lost a ten-year battle to brain cancer in 1990, Rick was left with unparalleled despair but also the greatest lesson anyone could communicate—one that resounds the power of courage, strength, fighting spirit, and human relationships. It was the very epitome of the big picture that so many of us tend to lose sight of, and it is an experience that touches Rick on all levels—personal, professional, and otherwise.

When talking business with Rick Toren, one might easily be intimidated by the plethora of technical knowledge and medical terminology peppering the recounts of his exploits. At once an expert salesman, healthcare administration expert, inventor, and entrepreneur, he is the very definition of a modern Renaissance man and exhibits extraordinary expertise across these fields. His underlying philosophy, however, is elegant in its simplicity and applicable to anyone, regardless of their age or profession. When you make up your mind to take a shot at something, no amount of practice swings will get you there. It's only when you commit to the stroke and make contact with the ball that you have any chance at success. Sometimes the goal is achieved and sometimes it isn't, but as long as we are honest with ourselves and honor the rules of the game, we can draw support and inspiration from our family, friends, and mentors. So work hard, play smart, and most importantly, add heart.

BERNHARDT
WEALTH MANAGEMENT

Daniel Turner

Delegating by Design

What should people know about Dan Turner? "I'm bald," he proclaims. "Really bald."

Dan's dry humor and casual confidence are readily apparent, but the complex personality under that bald pate, and the traits that enabled him to turn a $10,000 contract into a $10 million company specializing in IT problem-solving for Federal agencies, are less obvious. From the time he sold bottles of Snapple out of his locker in junior high school, undermining the school's vending machine revenues until the school's administration shut down his operation, Dan has distinguished himself as an entrepreneur. Now the Founder and President of TCG, it's certain that there's more to know about Dan Turner than his bald head.

TCG is a government contractor specializing in IT, grants management, budget formulation and execution, and the creation of grantee communities, anticipating $10 million in revenue this year. The company's

35 employees and 22 contractors principally work in the DC metropolitan area. Its first contract was to develop iEdison for the National Institute of Health (NIH) to allow grantees to report patents. Dan designed the program with his college roommate in a house in Pennsylvania in 1995. iEdison is now used by the entire Federal government, and it set TCG on its course of expertise in innovative IT solutions and direction. The company has since earned renown through recognition on the Inc. 500/5000 list, and one of its projects recently won the 2009 Excellence.Gov Award for "best overall," honoring its commitment to transparency.

Dan grew up as the oldest of three children and enjoyed the influence of a father who was self-employed as a Clinical Psychologist. Aside from the insightful relational skills he learned from his dad—skills that would later equip him with valuable managerial insight—Dan saw what it was like to be your own boss. Furthermore, Dan grew up a self-proclaimed geek. "I was a geek before there were geeks," he laughs now. In 1980, his mother was a freelance journalist and had a column called "All About Computers," which examined and chronicled the personal computer revolution. As a result, Dan grew up in a very different kind of environment than the vast majority of his peers. While most households saw modern technological devices like computers as a luxury, his mother was always receiving the latest designs and models to test and critique.

"We had a variety of early Macs," Dan recalls, "and we had one of the first laser printers with all these radiation warning signs posted on it." He learned early about technology and became comfortable with it long before his peers or teachers were even prepared to accept it. He wielded this proficiency not only as a tool to improve his efficiency and aesthetic presentation in school, but also to impress the ladies when the occasion arose.

When he was old enough, Dan also leveraged his then-unique knowledge to earn money. When a local religious leader needed someone to compile a database of songs, he knew that Dan Turner, then 11, was the man for the job. Nevertheless, Dan did not at the time consider a career in computers. As a child, he got to know a globetrotting economist and was determined to follow in his footsteps. However, when he entered college and failed his first economics course, he knew it was time to switch gears. His college roommate was working toward a dual degree in math and computer science, and Dan couldn't help but notice his fascinating assignments. Thus, in the midst of his sophomore year, Dan added a computer science major to his creative writing degree.

Unlike most businesses, TCG was founded accidentally. Dan graduated from college three months late after failing calculus four times and taking it in summer school. Once he received his degree, he sought employment at the NIH, where he had worked the three previous summers. No jobs were available, however, so he sent his resume to a few other companies. He was surprised when, two weeks later, NIH contacted him about a $10,000 contract that was open for bidding. With his experience in computer programming in college and his comparatively low rates, they thought he might be a good fit. Dan won the six-month project, but quickly realized that his skill set was a poor match for the project's requirements. Instead of throwing in the towel, however, he contacted his college roommate, who at that time was working toward his PhD in computer science at the University of Pennsylvania. Dan hired him to do the technical work, which was completed within a month.

When the project was submitted to NIH, the young entrepreneur was informed that it had only been a prototype and that he and his former roommate were to now commence on the actual product. They then received a $25,000 contract, and TCG was born.

Now, sixteen years down the road, Dan is running a virtual business in which the majority of his staff telecommutes or works on clients' sites. Cohesion and solidarity are maintained through daily, weekly, annual, and quarterly meetings to ensure that plans, goals, and actions are properly and effectively aligned. Dan also relies on his management team—composed of the Head of Business Development, the CTO/CIO, the Head of Project Managers, and the Head of Recruiting and Process—to maintain effective leadership.

This reliance on others goes back to his initial delegation of tasks to his old roommate. Thus, TCG started as a delegated-responsibility company, and Dan's ability to know his own limitations and to act accordingly remain among his most unique and powerful management techniques. "The only true wisdom is in knowing you know nothing," proclaimed the Greek philosopher Socrates. Dan applies the philosophy to TCG by hiring experts to bring in their experience and knowledge and then letting them do their magic. This frees up his time so he can focus on the more abstract and long-term visions for TCG. For example, Dan hired his mother three years after starting the company when he realized he was no good at project management. "The goal of being a business owner is to make yourself obsolete," he explains. "Right now I'm about to delegate my last two daily tasks so I can focus on getting new business, strategic planning, systematization, and the culture of the company."

In addition to this philosophy of compartmentalization, Dan prides himself on TCG's ability to unearth solutions where others might see problems. TCG's mantra has always been "Yes, it *can* be done!" First and foremost, the business is built around its ability to solve problems that impede their customers. "We have the advantage of an outside perspective, and we've seen multiple customers go through the same problem. This is where our value lies," says Dan.

The ability to problem-solve and strategize despite obstacles can be traced back to Dan's mother, who was known for a key piece of advice: "Use all your resources." The adage forged unparalleled sleuthing skills in her young son, which have evolved into superior research and investigative talents in his adult years. "Whenever there is a problem, I know where to look to find the answer," he explains. "I can fix programs based on certain assumptions that tend to be accurate." In this manner, it becomes irrelevant whether Dan himself knows the answer to a question, as it is attainable regardless. Being able to quickly get his hands on any answer he needs means his clients get he benefit of an expansive and comprehensive knowledge base.

Dan orients his management style around conservative financial stratagems aimed at maintaining the fundamental integrity of TCG. "I think in cash basis," he concedes. "My whole life is cash basis. If it's not cash, it doesn't exist." This attitude might be traced back to his interest in educating himself about business. He spoke to other contractors, who helped him develop a spreadsheet to identify and analyze the sources of cost in his business. He also joined the Young Entrepreneurs' Organization, now the Entrepreneurs' Organization (EO), a worldwide educational enterprise supporting the development and empowerment of entrepreneurs and their companies. The organization provided informal mentoring and later became Dan's informal advisory board. "It was a key component in the evolution of my business because it gave me people to talk to who could really understand and relate to me," he explains.

Despite his entrepreneurship and his outstanding success as a business founder, Dan says that his true passion lies not in the groundwork of building a company but rather in its subsequent structuring and maintenance. "I actually didn't like starting the business," he admits. "What I like most is running it. I love getting up every day and doing payroll or bookkeeping, though I will soon be delegating these aspects as well." Sixteen years into the business, he now wants to step beyond the day-to-day operation of the company so he can direct his resources toward more strategic endeavors.

As TCG proclaims in its core tenets, it is oriented around intelligence, value, emotional investment, collaboration, honesty, and family. Dan, too, does not fret too much about maintaining a certain style of discipline or leadership. "Our mission is to save time for the client," Dan emphasizes. "This is the bottom line."

Dan's advice to entrepreneurs entering the business world today is essentially based on Maslow's hierarchy of needs, suggesting that they find a job and maintain it until their basic needs are met. Once shelter and food are provided for, they can focus on self-fulfillment. Dan's first contract came while he was still living with his parents, and he could save money. With this foundational cornerstone in place, other young entrepreneurs could also transform first opportunities into full-fledged businesses. It just takes initiative, skill, collaboration, understanding, and the ability to find the right people and to be willing to delegate to them. "And luck," says Dan. "Lots of luck."

Jerry Wolman

A Little Luck, A Lot of Love

Shifting nervously, Jerry Wolman's elbow slid sideways a few inches across the loan officer's desk. A single penny had been in its path and was sent tumbling to the floor in the process, rolling under the desk and out of sight. Engrossed in his work, the loan officer paid little heed to the lost change and instead focused his attention on the request at hand—an appeal for five thousand dollars he would have to deny based on the bank's requirements and policies. Jerry, however, knelt down to his knees and reached under the desk to retrieve the coin. He returned it to its rightful place on the desk and sat back in his chair to await his fate.

Popular culture mandates that picking up a penny brings good luck, but rarely does this fortune come so obviously and quickly after the act is performed. Looking up from his work in time to notice the subtle deed, the officer froze for a moment, considered, and then extended his hand in a congratulatory gesture.

"Jerry, anyone that's going to worry about my penny is going to worry about my five thousand dollars. The loan is yours," he said.

Knowing the officer was sticking his neck out in a generous act of good faith, Jerry couldn't believe the news. Having recently struck out on his own to pursue a career in real estate, the loan would allow him to purchase the piece of property he had in mind for his first project. Securing the loan was the first step in what proved to be a lengthy and taxing process of obtaining proper financing, permits, subcontractors, and architects, but the incident with the loan officer demonstrated the compelling combination of luck and kindness that would ultimately lead Jerry to overwhelming success. "The harder I worked, the luckier I got," he says now, looking back on his incredible journey and lending true weight to the penny's symbolism. "You need luck, of course, but you have to work hard to obtain this luck. You have to be in the right places at the right time and take advantage of the opportunities that come up."

When he started in the construction industry, Jerry had no worth statement, no background, and no experience. He was just a humble, self-taught painter from Shenandoah, Pennsylvania trying to make his way in Washington, D.C. Nowadays, when people hear the name Jerry Wolman, it's hard to guess what accomplishment will come to mind first.

Will it be his dramatic transformation from the boy who couldn't afford tickets to see Philadelphia Eagles games into the man who purchased the team? Will it be the fact that he was the founding owner of the Philadelphia Flyers professional hockey team, the owner of the Connie Mack Stadium, developer of the Spectrum arena, and a pivotal player in building the Philadelphia Veterans Stadium? Will it be his incredible contribution to Chicago's skyline through the development and ownership of the John Hancock Center, or his incredible contribution to D.C.'s urban development through his ownership of the National Theatre and the Federal Building? Over his lifetime, Jerry developed more than two and a half million square feet of office and retail space and eight hundred apartment units in Chicago, thirty thousand apartment units in the D.C. metro area, and over five million square feet of office space in D.C. as well. Or perhaps one will instead recall the decrescendo of his wealth as his financial empire, valued at $100 million, swiftly evaporated after a faulty construction deal. Regardless of what one thinks of first, the impact of Jerry's lifetime cannot truly be grasped unless one starts with the very first chapter.

Jerry's incredible story begins in a small coal-mining town in 1927, where he was born to a family of modest material means but tremendous love and integrity. Though many would argue that the odds were against him from day one, he insists that it was quite the opposite, as his small-town upbringing bred a work ethic that is rarely produced by other settings. As one of nine children, his father put him to work at age five at the wholesale produce company he owned, and Jerry recalls a strong urge to earn money to contribute to his family's wellbeing. Edward Bennett Williams, attorney to the President of the Washington Redskins, would sum up his sentiment perfectly in a conversation many years later when he said, "Jerry, they'll never beat guys like you and me. We'll always come back for one reason: we have the luxury of coming from poverty."

Days were busy for the young boy, who would put in hours of work at the warehouse before and after school. At age twelve, Jerry would purchase crates of oranges from his father and then sell them from a wagon he pulled from house to house, earning enough money to buy sodas, ice cream, and movie tickets after giving a portion of his earnings to his mother. After an extremely brief stint plucking chickens at a butcher shop in which he got through only one bird, he drove a truck for his father starting at age fourteen. Amidst the demands of his employment, Jerry still found time to hitchhike with his best friend Johnny Robel, traveling the hundred miles separating him from his favorite sports team, the Philadelphia Eagles. With his face pressed eagerly up to the bars of the stadium gate, he befriended a guard who would often let him in at half time to watch the rest of the game. "Football was the only game that was really in our blood," he says now. Though he couldn't play himself because his family depended on him to work, his passion and enthusiasm for the game remained strong and pervasive.

Despite the manual labor of his jobs thus far, Jerry gave considerable thought to his future and had decided by his senior year of high school that he hoped to become an attorney or a rabbi. His dreaming came to an abrupt halt, however, when his father had a stroke that left him incapacitated. Jerry had to drop out of high school to work and support his family, leaving behind his beloved teachers and studies.

Thankfully, his father eventually recovered enough to return to work, and at seventeen years of age, Jerry was again free to follow the calling of his exceptionally large heart. America had recently entered the Second World War, and a patriotic spirit had permeated its cities and countryside. Jerry finally convinced his friend Johnny to run away with him to join the navy—a feat his parents would have forbidden otherwise. Jerry flunked his physical but then attended officer training school for the Merchant Marines and was deployed thirty days later, laying eyes on a ship for the first time in his life. He served with the Merchant Marines for about two years shuttling troops over to France, holding true to his sense of duty until the war's end.

It was shortly thereafter that Jerry returned to Shenandoah. A lifelong flirt and charmer, he and his brother Bernard would sometimes travel to a nearby town in search of dates—pretty girls with high cheekbones like Gene Tierney, among the most beautiful actresses of the time. One day, the brothers traveled to Wilkes-Barre and accidentally stumbled into a wedding reception at the town's Jewish Community Center when Jerry's eyes landed on a girl standing across the room—a girl with high cheekbones and a certain way about her. "Bernie, do you see that girl?" he said to his brother. "I'm going to marry her." A year later, he did.

Jerry and Anne Wolman had much in common. They held the same values, both wanted children, and both shared a marvelous trust in the world that came in handy when Jerry realized he couldn't make a living in Wilkes-Barre, even after he opened a small fruit stand. After drawing a blank as to where to relocate, Jerry was suddenly struck with an inspired idea. "Anne, we've got a '38 Chevy and not much else," he said. "Why don't we pack the car and pick up a hitchhiker, and wherever he's going, that's where we'll stay?" The young couple kissed, packed the car, bid farewell to their families, and set out to Mountain Top, Pennsylvania, where they picked up a hitchhiker bound for school in Washington, D.C. "You've got a ride," they told him, and they had their destination.

"We must have had a dollar or less," says Jerry, recalling their arrival in the city. "We went to a Hot Shoppe, split a hot fudge sundae, and bought a newspaper to look for a room." They followed an advertisement to Fifth Street, where a woman by the name of Mrs. O'Hara had a room available for ten dollars. They told her they'd like to take it and intended to go downtown the next day to get jobs, asking if they could pay her once they received their first paycheck. "That's fine," said the kindly woman, who promptly called the grocery store across the street and requested thirty dollars' worth of credit for the young couple that she would guarantee. Exhibiting much the same faith and benevolence that the loan officer would convey several years later, Jerry's ability to inspire trust and kinship in his fellow human beings was uncanny even from the beginning.

The next day, Anne got a job at Prudential Life Insurance Company and Jerry at Colonial Wallpaper and Paint Company, swiftly picking up the art of trimming wallpaper and mixing colors. He was swiftly promoted to store manager, raising profits steeply by revolutionizing the company's manner of bookkeeping and customer service. As he waited patiently for the bonus the company's owner had promised him, Jerry would sell paint to a nearby construction site and couldn't help but observe with transfixed fascination as they poured concrete, raised walls, and threaded electrical wiring. "I was turned on by the whole process," he reminisces. "You're doing something only men and God could do: constructing buildings and seeing people move into them."

Shortly thereafter, Jerry submitted his resignation after two years at the company to go into business for himself. He worked as a painter to support his young family as he began to learn the ins and outs of the development world, and it wasn't long before he had earned a name for himself as the Boy Wonder of real estate, leaving an incredibly large and permanent footprint on the histories of development and sports alike.

While Jerry's monetary fortune pursued a rollercoaster course from rags to riches and back to rags again, his incredible fortune of love and perseverance remained constant throughout it all. His two children, Helene and Alan, and nine grandchildren are his best friends, and after Anne's untimely death, he remarried a lovely woman named Bobbie, adding another best friend to the mix. Now, at the age of eighty-three, Jerry can often be found texting or Facebook messaging with his grandchildren, his inbox routinely populated with little "I love you" reminders.

A life as rich as Jerry's undoubtedly presents a treasure trove of lessons, and he doesn't hesitate to teach just as freely as he loves. "The best lesson I learned in the development business is that time is money," Jerry says. "Also, if you're making money, take care of the people you're working with. You can't get anywhere without these people, and beyond this, there's nothing better than sharing the wealth," he confirms. He is known for always gifting interest in his projects to the people who helped him achieve success, never once maintaining complete ownership.

Despite the myriad of ups and downs that color his life's canvas, Jerry's main regret stems back to the foundation of it all—the fact that he was unable to finish high school. "There's nothing more important than an education," he emphasizes now. "Had I been able to finish high school and attend college, I probably would have been able to avoid some of the pitfalls I endured."

Beyond these articulated teachings, Jerry is even more so a lesson in his simple existence. He is, above all else, an expert in what it means to truly be human—in the compassion, kindness, generosity, and love that makes life worth living. He brings the best out in people, compelling each one of us to care greater, laugh louder, and love deeper, inspiring a sincerity that many of us didn't even know we had.

Furthermore, he is a connoisseur at the practice of both exhibiting and receiving generosity. Mrs. O'Hara, the kindly landlady who helped him in good faith at the outset of his journey, received flowers on Mother's Day until her death. Reporters who used to criticize and doubt him have since been transformed into friends through his good humor and patience. His expansive list of charity work has been done largely anonymously, and his generosity toward friends and strangers alike has been unparalleled and unquestioning.

"My real joy in life, however, is being with my family," he confirms. "They're the impetus for all that I've done and all that I will do." Jerry's affection for his family extends even to the more universal family of human kind, a web of which we're all apart. "I don't think people realize how much I love *people*," he says, his statement forming an umbrella over all of humanity. He speaks badly of nobody and behaves in a parallel manner. "Treat people the way you'd like to be treated," he says, echoing the old adage with a fervency and conviction that infuses new life into the words. "Never believe you're better than anybody else and always be humble," he adds. And above all, Jerry stresses, "Always follow your dreams."

So after hearing a more complete version of the story, what comes to mind when one hears the name Jerry Wolman? Perhaps we are reminded of our own families and the importance of showing our gratitude for them each and every day. Perhaps it is the strangers we meet along the path of life and the importance of demonstrating kindness and generosity regardless of wealth or stature. Or perhaps it is simply a more complete, encompassing, enduring idea of love—one that is kind even to its adversaries, giving even if it has nothing, and brimming with hope, integrity, humility, and staying power. If one ever needed proof that such ideals can translate into reality, there's Jerry.

Sonny Younce

Incremental Progress, Immense Success

There is a good reason why Rome wasn't built in a day, and Sonny Younce understands it perfectly. Through small yet steady steps toward success, he was able to revive A-Annandale, Inc., from the brink of bankruptcy and transform it into a thriving and competitive business. Now among the largest highway marking companies in Northern Virginia, the company enjoys $7.6 million in revenue with aims to double that number in the near future. By embracing diversification and launching new divisions, Younce employs an unwavering work ethic and a revitalized workforce to lead the company toward new horizons.

A-Annandale was founded in 1982 by Jim Whitney, a pioneer in the highway marking industry. Though exceptionally skilled in the field, Whitney had little interest in acting as a manger and didn't place much emphasis on running the company. As a result, the company depreciated in value during each of the twenty-five years leading up to Sonny's involvement. This decline culminated in 2005, when one of its workers was fatally injured on the job. With workman's compensation and general liability coverage skyrocketing and with the sudden and premature death of Whitney himself, Sonny arrived in June of 2007 to what he describes as "a madhouse." Whitney had left the company to his sister, who had little working knowledge of construction or accounting matters. With $4 million in debt and only marginal profits, the future for A-Annandale looked bleak indeed. Sonny's wife had been Ms. Whitney's nurse for several years, and when the distraught woman spoke to Mrs. Younce of her need for a president to run her asphalt marking company, she knew Sonny was just the man for the job.

When Sonny first assumed his position with A-Annandale, he faced stark opposition and friction from the workforce. Wary of an outsider who proposed to revolutionize the established order of the company's procedures, they even plotted against their new president as he struggled to keep the company afloat. "When I came in the door, I introduced myself and you could actually feel the tension in the space," he marvels. Indeed, Sonny's first order of business was a thorough audit of company documentation and practice to cut the budget wherever possible. He slashed overtime and expenditures, ultimately saving the company $600,000 in seven months. "It wasn't one big thing that I did," he explains, "but a slew of little things which added up to this big sum."

Sonny again exhibited his commitment to incremental, bite-sized progressions through his investment in new machinery. In their early jobs, he recalls arriving on location for a prime contractor just to face the embarrassment of their out-dated and failing equipment. When faced with so many setbacks, leaders are oftentimes paralyzed by the sheer magnitude of their obstacles. Sonny, however, knew that the process of rejuvenation had to begin somewhere, so he decided to start with buying one new truck. "It was like kids seeing their first toy, it was so shiny and new," he recalls of his workforce. The pride and relief emanating from his once-begrudging team was tangible, and he leveraged the sentiment to establish a new camaraderie. "If you listen to what I tell you and do what I say, we'll change this company together," he had declared. "We'll have a vision. If you work hard for me, I'll work hard for you." Henceforth, he noticed change sweeping through A-Annandale one worker at a time. Each man became more company-oriented, arriving on time and willing to go the extra mile. They had always been a professional company, but the lack of structure and vision had left morale low. Sonny's impact, however, changed everything.

Though fraught with success, Sonny's message remains a humble one. "If I can do this, anybody can," he insists. "I don't have a college education. I just pulled from all the folks I had worked under, who were all very smart people. They were mentors and I'm grateful for them." Though he had initially resented these mentors for their high standards and strict expectations, he notes a seminal moment in which a "light clicked" and he realized that he was surrounded by brilliant people from which to learn and grow. With thirty-four years of industry experience under his belt today, one can only imagine the countless lessons he has accumulated by maintaining this open frame of mind.

All these lessons began in Tennessee, where Sonny accepted his first job out of high school with the road building company where both his father and grandfather had been employed. Founded in 1932 amidst the turmoil of the depression, it seemed as though each of its four hundred plus employees was personally committed to the company's mission and goals. Beginning in a very basic position of general laborer, Sonny worked his way up and eventually found himself employed in the pavement marking division at age twenty-seven—an area he felt particularly drawn to. He felt as though his freshly-painted roads were works of art with a beauty all their own. Then, when his supervisor passed away suddenly, he was promoted to a supervisory position. It was at that point that a more formal mentoring relationship crystallized between himself and the general superintendent, who taught him an array of skills. Sonny learned how to approach his crew, how to formally present himself and his strategies in meetings, and how to approach the logistical aspects of a job so as to maximize profit. "Quality work and timely work got me to where I am today," he reports.

Ready to press the limits of his capabilities, he decided to strike out on his own in 1995 and distributed his resume all across the U.S. to advertise his services as a consultant. The response was lavish, and he quickly accumulated a number of clients. "I saw purpose in what I was doing," he says. "Not only was I training them, but I was learning something about myself; that I had the ability to drive, to change, to influence." Then, armed with "nothin' but some clothes and a promise," Sonny reports, he and his future wife accepted positions in Alaska, Las Vegas, and Seattle. Their openness to experience and transition evidences a unique flexibility of character that allowed them to make the most of each experience that came their way, especially when they received the call from Ms. Whitney. When they heard about the opportunity for Sonny at A-Annandale in 2007, they hopped in the car and drove across the country to take up residence in Northern Virginia, where they currently reside.

After working for A-Annandale for several months and realizing the tremendous amount of discipline and focus it would take to turn the company around, he made an offer of purchase to Ms. Whitney in September of 2008. Once she expressed interest, he set about the tedious process of securing a loan from the bank. He recalls a tightening in his chest as the experience unfolded. "Knowing you're at the threshold of living a dream, it's like looking through a cloud," he explains. "You can't quite touch it, but you know it's there." Sonny also notes that, on the day the loan closed, the market fell nine hundred points. In retrospect, he marvels, "I'm most proud of being able to operate in an upside down economy and survive." Indeed, he threw his utmost effort into his work and turned a profit of $550,000 in his first year of ownership, even after expenditures.

Sonny's tremendous focus and tenacity can be attributed in large part to his father, who had also dreamed of owning his own company. This dream, however, unraveled into a nightmare, and Sonny watched as he struggled to form a company that ultimately failed after seven years of hardship. A teenager at the time, Sonny learned that owning your own company is much larger than one's expertise in an industry. Taxes, insurance, contracts, and verbiage complicate the equation. His father had all the skill in the world, but his fatal flaw was his failure to analyze business logistics, and Sonny was committed to salvage this lesson from the misfortune.

Beyond careful analysis and monitoring, Sonny's ultimate goal as a leader and president is to enforce accountability, which he accomplishes through thorough documentation. Such practices provide a blueprint for increasing productivity and for identifying key employees who are truly dedicated to the company's success. To Sonny, this entails a purity of motive and an ability to look at the larger picture. To young entrepreneurs, he advises, "Don't look at a business as 'I'm going to get rich and famous.' Go into it with love and heart and do your research. Don't leave one stone unturned. Go in with all the knowledge you can possibly have, and when you get into the seat, don't ever assume that you're on top and don't have to work as hard. Because really, you have to work harder to keep it going. Don't ever think failure. Figure out a solution. If plan A don't work, go to plan B."

Beyond these recommendations, Sonny's story confirms again and again the significance of each step toward a goal, no matter how small. Whether it's the first purchase of a new piece of machinery or the first dollar paid back to a $4 million debt, he lends truth to the concept that a thousand mile journey truly starts with a single step. "Entrepreneurship is just about taking one step," he confirms. So, considering how many steps we each take in a day, why not make just one towards a dream?

About the Author

Having grown up on a farm in Nebraska, Gordon Bernhardt left the Midwest in the early 1980s for Washington D.C. to work as an assistant in the U.S. House of Representatives. He left behind the rural lifestyle but he carried with him the values of hard work, a focus on what you can control, and service to others—values that continue to influence his life, today.

After completing a bachelor's degree in Commerce at the University of Virginia, Bernhardt began a successful career in finance at a leading accounting firm and two different brokerage companies. In 1994, in order to make the kind of difference in people's lives that he hoped to make, he established Bernhardt Wealth Management, an independent registered investment advisory firm built on the principle of fiduciary care: providing investment and wealth management guidance, service, and advice that places clients' interests and needs ahead of everything else. By adhering to this higher standard, he removed the conflicts of interest that were prevalent elsewhere. Rather than be restricted by a large company's cookie cutter methodology, he and his team are able to create customized plans that are far more appropriate for individual clients. Today, Bernhardt Wealth Management is recognized as one of the top fee-only wealth management firms in the Washington D.C. region.

In addition to being an entrepreneur and wealth manager, Bernhardt is the author of *Buen Camino: What a Hike through Spain Taught Me about Investing and Life*, a memoir about the 35-day, 618-mile pilgrimage he completed in Spain and the lessons he learned along the way. He also writes a weekly finance blog. Bernhardt writes the *Profiles in Success: Inspiration from Executive Leaders* book series, and hosts a podcast with the same name, to expand the influence of outstanding leaders while inspiring the next generation of executives.

Find out more about Gordon Bernhardt at
www.BernhardtWealth.com and www.ProfilesInSuccess.com.

Pvt. Jonathan Lee Gifford was the first U.S. soldier killed in Iraq. He was killed just two days into the war on March 23, 2003. Spc. David Emanual Hickman was killed by a roadside bomb in Iraq on November 14, 2011. *The Washington Post* on December 17, 2011, said Hickman "may have been the last" U.S. soldier killed in Iraq. After reading an article about Gifford and Hickman my sister, Gloria, was inspired to write the following poem.

From Gifford to Hickman

by Gloria J. Bernhardt

From Gifford to Hickman...and all those in between,
You fought bravely amid chaos and dangers unforeseen.
Twenty-one guns have sounded, the riderless horse walks on.
Fond memories are remaining. A nation's child is gone.

Sons and daughters; fathers, mothers—broken hearts intertwined.
Hugs and kisses; their successes—major milestones left behind.
Your selfless gift—a life laid down; for fellow soldier, family, land.
Duty called—call was answered—no greater love hath man.

"I'm getting taller. I lost a tooth. I got 100 on my test!
Miss your pancakes and your tickles, goodnight kisses were the best.
Who will answer all my questions now? I've important stuff to learn!
You said you had a big surprise on the day that you'd return."

"I talk to you at bedtime—after lights go out at night.
I told Jesus that I miss you...sure wish you could hug me tight.
When Grandpa says I look like you, Grandma starts to cry.
I'm mad that you're not coming home...I need to say goodbye!"

From Gifford, to Hickman, through every soldier who has served,
Liberty's fruits are savored and freedom is preserved.
We live freely due to soldiers, willing to support and defend
Our Constitution, our country—against enemies 'til the end.

Sons and daughters; fathers, mothers—broken hearts intertwined.
Hugs and kisses; their successes—major milestones left behind.
Your selfless gift—a life laid down; for fellow soldier, family, land.
Duty called—call was answered—no greater love hath man.

"I had a dream the night before...you smiled and walked on by.
When I awoke, I thought it odd...it seemed like a 'good-bye'.
I couldn't put my finger on the dark cloud that remained,
When the phone began to ring...I knew my life had changed."

"I questioned God, 'Why MY child? Why do I have to lose?'
I imagined His response would be 'If not your child, then whose?'
Your bright life flashed too briefly... seems He only takes the best.
I'm thankful for the time I had. For that I'm truly blessed."

From Gifford to Hickman and every warrior who has passed,
The price you've paid bought freedom, but will we make it last?
Your last breath drawn for citizens in this country and abroad
Are we worthy of such gifts is known only but to God.

Sons and daughters; fathers, mothers—broken hearts intertwined.
Hugs and kisses; their successes—major milestones left behind.
Your selfless gift—a life laid down; for fellow soldier, family, land.
Duty called—call was answered—no greater love hath man.

"My world stopped spinning…I couldn't breathe! Lord, how can I go on?
My days are all one midnight…but they say it's darkest 'fore the dawn.
I can hear you say, 'I'm proud of you! I know that this is hard.'
What do I do without you here? What dreams do I discard?"

"I miss your laugh. I miss your smell. I even miss our fights.
No more messes. No embraces. It's more 'real' late at night.
I saw you in a crowd today; but you vanished in the throng.
Wishful thinking changes nothing! I know my "rock" is gone."

FOR Gifford, FOR Hickman…FOR all the fallen in between,
You've trudged through shadowed valley and joined heroes' ranks unseen.
Upon freedom's altar, we sacrificed our daughters and our sons.
Empty boots stand at attention. The flag is folded. Your mission's done.

Made in United States
Orlando, FL
04 November 2026

90200513R00144